Talk Poetry

Poems and Interviews
with Nine American Poets

DAVID BAKER

A Kenyon Review Book

The University of Arkansas Press
Fayetteville • 2012

ISBN-10: 1-55728-981-6
ISBN-13: 978-1-55728-981-0

16   15   14   13   12   5   4   3   2   1

Text design by Ellen Beeler

♾ The paper used in this publication meets the minimum requirements of the
American National Standard for Permanence of Paper for Printed Library
Materials Z39.48-1984.

Library of Congress Cataloging-in-Publication Data

Baker, David, 1954-
    Talk poetry : poems and interviews with nine American poets / David Baker.
        p. cm.
    A Kenyon Review Book
    ISBN 978-1-55728-981-0 (pbk. : alk. paper)
    1. American poetry—21st century. 2. Poets, American—21st century—
    Interviews. 3. Poetry—Authorship. I. Title.
    PS617.B33 2012
    811'.608—dc23
                                                                        2011047592

I send a message by a Mouth that cannot speak—
  The Ecstasy to guess,
  Were a receipted Bliss
  If Grace could talk—
  —Emily Dickinson, unsent note to "Sweet Friends," 1885

Contents

Alice Notley

Meghan O'Rourke

Carl Phillips

Stanley Plumly

Arthur Sze

Preface

Poets are notoriously mute. They work alone. They fume and stew. They lean and loaf at their ease, writing the song of the self and by extension the songs of others. They seem to prefer the company of books.

But ask a poet about a poem, a favorite other poet, or anything having to do with their own work and habits and imagination, and you may find a real surprise: a bountiful font of conversation, enthusiasm, and explanation. They may tend to be loners and musers, but poets love to talk poetry. My poet friends even tell this story on themselves. If you have ever attended the popular Associated Writing Program's annual convention, it's certain you have seen those tables and tables of writers gesturing, arguing, intently talking. If they're talking about agents, you can bet those are fiction writers. If they're talking about movies, that's the playwrights. And the poets? It's line breaks and impersonal voice and disruption-versus-coherence and the superiority of metonymy over metaphor and . . . you get the point.

This has been the wellspring of *Talk Poetry*.

Talk Poetry gathers nine in-depth conversations with some of the most vibrant poets of our day. Each poet is engaged, passionate, and far-reaching in his or her views. It's also true that there are many kinds of poetry in America today. It would be folly to claim to represent that range with these, or any, nine poets. Yet I am delighted by the breadth you'll find here. Two of the poets (Fady Joudah and Meghan O'Rourke) had just published their first books when we conversed, while two others (Ted Kooser and W. S. Merwin) were serving as the nation's poet laureate during their interviews and, in fact, won the Pulitzer Prize during that tenure. That is, the poets in *Talk Poetry* range from emerging to major. There are other important divergent features among these poets in terms of background, regional affiliation, gender and sexual orientation, race and cultural identity, aesthetic taste and practice, and more. Many of the conversations probe such features.

So why these poets? I guess I'm not an objective observer in this project: I am an avid fan of each of them. To my mind each is doubly significant, representing an aesthetic field but also standing apart from the field. One friend has wondered to me how I can be so devoted to the poems of Alice Notley *and* Ted Kooser. They are, to my friend, the polar opposites of each other. But my answer is simple and firm. I do not believe an avant-garde style, or for that matter a baroque style, is the opposite of a plain style. The real opposite of a fine plain-style poem is a bad plain-style poem, just as the opposite of a superb experimentalist text is a bad one. Notley, Kooser, and the others here all stand together as examples of the capabilities of the art at its very best. As Arthur Sze says, "I'd rather advocate a diversity of aesthetics. We live in a time when the complexities of our planet require a diverse array of compelling imaginative poetry."

The present poets have a lot to say about poetry and—as it happens—about more than poetry. The contemporary poetry scene is heavily populated, wildly various, and at times downright heated. One of my hopes for this collection is to represent some of that variety, not through the mediating language of a critic but more directly in the words of poets themselves. Poetry criticism has its own peculiar malaise just now, and the poets here are refreshing for their passion and clarity, generally unaffiliated with camps and unburdened by the insular language of the contemporary university. As Alice Notley says in her interview, "poetry should feel hugely uncomfortable in the academy." W. S. Merwin seems to agree: "The arts are not about fulfilling some kind of academic obligation."

In fact, of these nine poets, five have never or have only on occasion taught in the university. Fady Joudah is a medical doctor who travels frequently with Doctors Without Borders. His moving testimony about medicine is matched here by his passion for the work of Mahmoud Darwish, the Palestinian poet whose work he translates. Meghan O'Rourke is a professional editor who has worked on the editorial boards of the *New Yorker* and the *Paris Review* and who currently serves as culture editor of *Slate*. Ted Kooser is retired from a career in the insurance industry, and his interview is full of practical business sense as well as of a passion for poetry's social possibilities; readers might enjoy comparing his experiences as poet laureate with W. S. Merwin's. Alice Notley speaks of the aesthetics of the immigrant and the avant-garde artist, and may surprise many readers with her opinion about the relation of poetry to critical theory: "Theory has nothing whatsoever to do with poetry."

If those five poets find their vocations outside the academy, Linda Gregerson, Carl Phillips, Stanley Plumly, and Arthur Sze are renowned for their teaching and are often sought out as academic workshop leaders and lecturers. Carl Phillips speaks with conviction about the "trusted community of writers" in a writing workshop. It's further significant that all four of these teachers bring a wide spectrum of pedagogical interests—including poetry writing—to their classrooms. Gregerson is a distinguished scholar of Renaissance studies, while Stanley Plumly is a leading authority on the life and works of John Keats. The more deeply Plumly delves into Keats, in our interview, the more intimately he seems to be unpacking his own aesthetic. Both Phillips and Sze make use of their important work as translators in their teaching—Greek and Latin for Phillips, Asian poetries for Sze. And of course few translators of our era have contributed more, and more widely, to the world's poetry than W. S. Merwin; his discussion extends from medieval French syllabics to the "creature" wisdom of John Clare to "irreducible" imagery in Asian poetry.

The poets of *Talk Poetry* range widely in their conversations—from politics to family life to the art of reading, from young Native American poets to old friends like John Berryman and Ted Berrigan. They are passionate about the environment, grade-school arts education, the value of the classics, and return time and again to probe the relation of poetry to painting, theater, film, popular culture, and so much more. As to their own styles, James Wright's "pure clear word" finds high value among some of these poets. But so do a number of contrary rhetorical designs—the impure word—from the gloss of the high baroque to the elusive post-structural trace. In fact, I think it's a particularly happy moment for poetry when formal and rhetorical choices don't automatically signal easy political ones, when the pure clear word finds value and avid readership, but the "unclear" word does, too.

There is more good news about our moment in poetic history. The Internet has added a vibrant dimension to publishing and the distribution of poetry. Small and independent presses release hundreds of books of poetry each year, e-magazines and blogs publish new and established poets of every aesthetic variety, and venues for public readings and workshops abound. There are more ways to find poetry, more places to hear it, and more types of publication and distribution than ever before. The contemporary university has provided a further kind of patronage of the art form, enabling a huge variety of poetics to flourish and to find voice and intellectual nurturing. In fact, to many observers, poetry has never been more rich, sought out, and various in our country's history.

But there are related perils, too. With the growth of Internet publishing and the incremental multiplication of social media, traditional bookstores are becoming an endangered species. Just this week Borders Books announced the decision to close its doors, all its doors, permanently. The independent bookstore, the literary bookstore, those genuine places where serious readers find real books—and attend readings, go to book-signings, and more—are in danger of extinction. This peril threatens to extend the distance between poets and readers who aren't poets. Ours is, further, a stifling cultural moment, when the arts and freedom of expression are beset by both political and economic stressors, yet a person can become a celebrity for the ability to throw a ball or, less, for no apparent reason at all. Far more people know Snooki Polizzi than Mark Strand.

Even within poetry, we face a vexing time when subcultures and special interests seem predominant. A young person may become a poet now by following a career path rather than out of soulful necessity. One can get a college major in creative writing, go on to earn an M.F.A. (or two) in creative writing, perhaps even attain a Ph.D. in creative writing with the expectation of further fellowships, residencies, and the eventual aspiration of teaching in a creative writing program. That is, one can become a professional writer without ever having left academia. The opportunities abound: institutional validation, professional tenure and advancement, the expectation of publication in magazines and books, grants, and a plethora of sanctioned places that provide time and quiet to write. So much networking, so many workshops. Sometimes being a poet feels less like a calling than an industry.

That is to say, the good news and the bad news are intricately bound. The poets of *Talk Poetry* tackle these and very many other subjects, conundrums, and opportunities. Following their dialogue is like sitting with them at a favorite café, late at night, listening, talking, and learning about this art form we all treasure.

I'd like to offer a few words about my process and aspiration for this project. I did not set out to conduct and compose a book of interviews with contemporary poets. In 2005 my friend and editor of the *Kenyon Review,* David Lynn, asked me if I would look through our forthcoming issues to see if I might interview one of the poets there about his or her poems for our new Web-based enterprise, Kenyon Review Online. I've served for more than fifteen years as poetry editor of the *Kenyon Review,* and my affiliation with the magazine goes back to 1984. Yet I hesitated when David issued his invitation. I'd never conducted an interview before (though I've given plenty). I do love talking to poets, though, so I agreed to try and quickly chose an exciting new poet, Meghan O'Rourke, with whom to talk. Since that first interview, KRO has received support from the National Endowment for the Arts to develop a series of such conversations, and these interviews have become one of KRO's defining features.

I have tried to engage each poet as a poet would like to be engaged—with a sense of background, context, and thorough preparation. I have myself been interviewed by people who clearly had not read my latest work . . . who hadn't read any of my work, for that matter, who never had heard of me. So—such interviews begin—tell me a little about yourself. What kind of poetry do you write? Who's your favorite poet? Did you have a pet, growing up? Did you hate your mother? I knew what I didn't want to do.

I also knew how I'd like to start. Each of these interviews commences with a discussion of particular poems—or in the case of Stanley Plumly, with a short section of prose, namely his Keats biography. Interviews very quickly turn foggy with generality. Rather than summarize each poet's work, we begin by looking together at specific texts, giving our conversation a focus and giving our readers a rare look at the poets' own feelings about these poems. I've included the actual poems and prose excerpts, so readers can follow the conversation easily and with precision. In fact, each of the opening texts was published in the *Kenyon Review* and provided me the first inspiration for the interviews themselves.

From here we move in all kinds of directions—into the poet's further projects and other interests, into discussions of other writers, into elements of autobiography, politics, and more. In each case it was a privilege to spend such extended time with such busy, engaged poets; every poet was generous and helpful as we talked, considered, and revised. Often our exchanges numbered in the several dozen over many months.

Some of these people are dear friends; some are slight acquaintances; one poet, Alice Notley, I have still not had the pleasure of meeting in person. I conducted most of the interviews through e-mail exchanges, with two exceptions. The interview with Ted Kooser was begun at Denison University, in March 2007, as a public conversation among Kooser, myself, and Tim Hofmeister, a longtime colleague and professor of classics at Denison. We later completed this interview by e-mail. The interview with W. S. Merwin was begun in the studios of Bloomberg News in New York City, in November 2010, as a video conversation among Merwin, David Lynn, and myself. This event was part of the tenth anniversary celebration of the Kenyon Review Lifetime Achievement Award, presented to Merwin in 2010. The video is still available through KRO. Merwin's print interview here is an edited and supplemented version of that video.

My gratitude to the nine poets here is immense. Their visions, brilliance, and generosity give this book its life and heart. To David Lynn, who first invited me to try an interview for the *Kenyon Review* and KRO, and whose friendship has buoyed me over the years, my deep thanks. To Larry Malley and colleagues at the University of Arkansas Press, it's such a pleasure to continue our long association. And finally, readers, my thanks to you for finding this book; I hope you are nourished by the feast of *Talk Poetry.*

Acknowledgments

These interviews were conducted with the support of the *Kenyon Review* and the National Endowment for the Arts. They were all published at the Kenyon Review Online. "Past the Centrality of Suffering: A Conversation with Fady Joudah" also appeared in the print version of the *Kenyon Review.* The poems, as well as Stanley Plumly's excerpt from "This Mortal Body," appear here with the permission of each of the poets and the magazine.

I am grateful to David Lynn and the staff of the *Kenyon Review* for their long support. To Denison University and the National Endowment for the Arts, again, my sincere appreciation.

Linda Gregerson

NINA SUBIN

LINDA GREGERSON was born in 1950 and raised in Cary, Illinois. She received her B.A. from Oberlin College, M.A. from Northwestern University, M.F.A. from the University of Iowa Writers' Workshop, and her Ph.D. from Stanford University. Currently she holds the Frederick G. L. Huetwell Professorship at the University of Michigan and teaches occasionally in the M.F.A. program for writers at Warren Wilson College. She also teaches frequently at the Kenyon Review Writers' Workshop, in Gambier, as well as at the Bread Loaf Writers' Conference.

Gregerson's poetry collections include *Fire in the Conservatory* (Dragon's Gate, 1982), *The Woman Who Died in Her Sleep* (Houghton Mifflin, 1996), *Waterborne* (Houghton Mifflin, 2002), *Magnetic North* (Houghton Mifflin, 2007), and *The Selvage* (Houghton Mifflin, 2012). For her poetry she has been awarded fellowships from the Guggenheim Foundation and the National Endowment for the Arts and an Academy Award in Literature from the American Academy of Arts and Letters, and she has received the prestigious Kingsley Tufts Poetry Prize, the Levinson Prize from *Poetry* magazine, and many other distinctions.

Gregerson's poetry is notable for the paradox of its rhetoric—at once literate and erudite, reaching into Renaissance tropes and subtle meters for depth, but also highly contemporary. A single poem may find her attentive to issues of neighborhood politics, global injustice, familial memory, and personal confession. This fusion of rhetorical intonations, narrative range, and formal varieties charges her work with notable power and distinctive energy.

In addition to the contributions of her poetry, Gregerson is an influential literary scholar. Her *The Reformation of the Subject: Spenser, Milton and the English Protestant Epic* appeared in 1995 from the Cambridge Studies in Renaissance Literature and Culture, and *Negative Capability: Contemporary American Poetry* was published in 2001 as part of the Poets on Poetry series from the University of Michigan Press.

Prodigal

Copper and ginger, the plentiful
    mass of it bound, half loosed, and
        bound again in lavish

    disregard as though such heaping up
were a thing indifferent, surfeit from
        the table of the gods, who do

        not give a thought to fairness, no,
    who throw their bounty in a single
lap. The chipped enamel—blue—on her nails.

The lashes sticky with sunlight. You would
    swear she hadn't a thought in her head
        except for her buttermilk waffle and

    its just proportion of jam. But while
she laughs and chews, half singing
        with the lyrics on the radio, half

        shrugging out of her bathrobe in the
    kitchen warmth, she doesn't quite
complete the last part, one of the

sleeves—as though, you'd swear, she
    couldn't be bothered—still covers
        her arm. Which means you do not

    see the cuts. Girls of an age—
fifteen for example—still bearing
        the traces of when-they-were

        new, of when-the-breasts-had-not-been-
    thought-of, when-the-troublesome-cleft-
was-smooth, are anchored

on a faultline, it's a wonder they
        survive at all. This ginger-haired
                darling isn't one of my own, if

own is ever the way to put it, but
I've known her since her heart could still
        be seen at work beneath

        the fontanelles. Her skin
    was almost other-worldly, touch
so silken it seemed another kind

of sight, a subtler
        boundary than obtains for all
                the rest of us, though ordinary

    mortals bear some remnant too,
consider the loved one's fine-
        grained inner arm. And so

        it's there, from wrist to
    elbow, that she cuts. She takes
her scissors to that perfect page, she's good,

she isn't stupid, she can see that we
        who are children of plenty have no
                excuse for suffering we

    should be ashamed and so she is
and so she has produced this many-
        layered hieroglyphic, channels

        raw, half-healed, reopened
    before the healing gains momentum, she
has taken for her copy-text the very

cogs and wheels of time. And as for
        her other body, says the plainsong
                on the morning news, the hole

in the ozone, the fish in the sea,
you were thinking what exactly? You
      were thinking a comfortable

      breakfast would help? I think
I thought we'd deal with that tomorrow.
Then you'll have to think again.

Over Easy

Cloud cover like a lid on.
      Thwarted trees. And three more hours
of highway to be rid of. My darlings don't want
        a book on tape. They want

a little indie rock, they want to melt
      the tweeters, they want
mama in the trunk so they can have some un-
        remarked-on fun.

Fine. I've got my window, I can contemplate
      the flatness of Ohio. I can think
about the ghastly things we've leached into
        the topsoil, I can marvel that the

scabrous fields will still accept the plow. Except
      some liquid thing is happening just behind
the trees, some narrow sub-
        cutaneous infusion where

the darkening earth and darker strato-
      cumulus have not yet sealed
their hold. A pooling
        fed by needle drip: pellucid, orange,

a tincture I would almost call unnatural were
      it not so plainly nature-
born. Till what had been a stricken contiguity
        of winter-wasted

saplings starts to sharpen and distill, as though
      a lens had been adjusted or a mind
had cleared. Our sorry dispersal,
        the Bishop of Africa wrote

to his flock, but the voice of a child
    recalled me. When the girls were small
we took them to an island once, the sun
      above the sea, and with

the other paying customers we'd watch it set.
    A yolk, I thought. The not-yet-
torn meniscus with its cunning corrective to
      up and down. You've held

one in your palm no doubt: remember the weight?
    Remember the lemony slickness we so oddly
call "the white" and how it drains
      between your fingers? Not

in chambering and wantonness the sun would swell
    nor strife and plumply flatten like
a yolk-in-hand. Would steep there in the salt-
      besotted vapors till

we must have been watching an aftereffect,
    so quickly did it vanish. Till
the whole of expectation, wrote the bishop—this
      Ohio sky, the road, my noisy

darlings—is exhausted and—
    now mandarin, madder—what was
the future—cinnabar, saffron, marigold,
      quince—becomes the past.

So I Go to Words

A Conversation with Linda Gregerson

David Baker: Linda, thanks so much for the chance to talk about these two poems of yours. They are splendid poems, both of them. I'd also like to use this occasion to talk about your recent book of poems, *Magnetic North,* and to range further into other interests of yours, like teaching, Renaissance poetry and scholarship, the theater, more.

But let's start with "Over Easy." This is one of my favorite later poems of yours. I have a few specific questions about this poem, but I wonder if there's anything you wish to say about it first—about its origin or impetus or whatever you might wish to say to begin.

Linda Gregerson: Well, in the first place, you are very kind to overlook the speaker's comments on the Ohio landscape, not to hold them against me, I mean. And I should also say I regard that landscape—northern Ohio, northern Illinois, southern Wisconsin, southern Michigan, not the lushness and lovely elevations of points further south and north, but the sectioned-off flatness of farmlands and shopping malls—as my unerasable imaginative home. But yes, the origins: a car trip, and perhaps the purest sensuous incitement I've ever tried to get down on paper. At which I flatly failed, by the way. It was that radiant sliver of limpid tangerine: I could taste it in the back of my throat, and it brought such pure enchantment. Midwestern Proust. I spent ages trying to identify the sense-memory, which was multiple and mildly mortifying: a dress I had in high school, a pair of fishnet stockings, a lipstick (it was the sixties, remember; we *all* looked ghastly!), and a sort of sherbet-on-a-stick we used to call a "Push-Up." Quite a farrago, and of course I had to ditch it all. But I tried to keep the impetus, that primitive thing that comes before speech and way before aesthetic judgment.

DB: There are things in "Over Easy" that resonate with your larger body of work—the family narrative, the voice concurrently tender and intellectual, the persisting turn toward conscience or toward something like social connection or civic adhesion. But rarely in your poems is the speaker, simply, moving. Have you noticed? Here she's in her car with her daughters, blasting the stereo, as they range across those "scabrous fields" of Ohio. Your poems are nearly always underscored by a tension between velocity and impediment, to be sure; but the velocity is usually intellectual. In "Over Easy" it's also literal, physical. She is on the move.

LG: Ah, you *don't* overlook the comment on the landscape! But you're right about the movement, and I'm afraid it doesn't speak well of me that I'm so rarely able to imagine a speaker in physical motion. I suffer from the can't-chew-gum-and-walk syndrome: it takes something remarkable to make me notice the world if I'm trying to move through it. The beginning of the poem is meant to be more than a little at my own expense.

DB: I guess I asked about movement because I think one of the central things about this poem is its trope of dispersal, "our sorry dispersal." Physical movement and losing control—like that important image of the egg, broken and running. This is the anxiety or the fear over a loss of influence. So much speed, so much time passing quickly. It's also the parents' abiding nightmare, isn't it?

LG: I'm not sure I'd call it "nightmare," though God knows nothing makes one feel the passage of time more keenly than staking one's heart to a child. But your larger insight is deeply right: beneath the domestic comedy is meant to be something darker. It's an appalling confession the speaker makes, to wish to "be rid of" any parcel of time in this brief life, and yet we do it all the time. Perhaps the fear of tedium is one of the most durable legacies of scabrous fields.

But I cannot blame the fields for my own failures of attention. The Reformers I study in the other part of my life would have said that boredom is a sin, and that seems to me to be much closer to the truth. "Sorry dispersal" is Augustine. Or rather, it's Augustine by way of a marvelous essay by Margaret Ferguson; the other italicized parts of the poem are Augustine altogether. I felt quite *driven* to Augustine as I tried to capture that preternatural transition of sunset and silhouette. There's a passage in the eleventh book of the *Confessions* where the author writes a sort of phenomenology of time. His example is the recitation of a psalm, the passage of the verse through expectation, attention, and memory. I think it's no accident he draws his example from a sacred poem. The great mystery, of course, is that cusp we call the present, which has always escaped me, except, perhaps, in the context of a poem or the voice of a child. The keenest edge of mortality, yes, but blessing rather than nightmare.

DB: Perhaps blessing *and* nightmare? That seems to be the dynamic tension that turns inside your work. "Over Easy" is remarkable for its turnings, as one scene, one image, one idea, morphs into the next. You seem to do such things so naturally. I know, Yeats's lesson in "Adam's Curse" reminds us that the natural is an achievement of great labor. The apparent ease with which you turn your poems must be a result of that kind of work.

"Prodigal" offers an even more stunning transfiguration. How can a young woman, a girl with such plenty and such hope, be driven to such hopeless or impoverished behavior? The first magic of the poem derives from how you adjust her portrait from "the plentiful mass" of her hair to the shock of her cutting herself.

LG: Cutting, anorexia, all these ghastly varieties of self-harm: they are not chiefly practiced by children who cannot get enough to eat or have just seen their village burned by hostile forces; they are diseases of plenty. And they are real. Real suffering. We cannot make them go away by pointing to their unreasonableness.

DB: This poem connects in my imagination to others of your poems that represent, and speak in behalf of, the young in their afflictions. In "The Resurrection of the Body" we witness a young helmeted boy, bashing his head against the wall of his hospital room; in "For the Taking" we find a young girl sexually abused by her "bad uncle." Elsewhere there are children ill, stricken, helpless, speechless. Here you render such pathos and tenderness ("I've known her since her heart could still / be seen at work beneath // the fontenelles") for the young cutter. The tension of paradox again: Her fortunate lot in life, this well-to-do American girl, is also the cause of her shame and her suffering. Would you like to speak to this major impulse in your poetry?

LG: One of my friends, a sociologist, said to me once in another context (she was teaching a course on Disability and the State) that a culture can be measured by the way it treats its most vulnerable members. Somewhere prior to analysis, somewhere very elemental indeed, I feel the world can be measured by how it treats its children. I cannot bear the harm we do to them; it makes me wild with grief. And there's nowhere else to go with such grief—I mean one can, one must, try to do some practical good in the world but it's always such a pittance—so I go to words.

DB: Words indeed. The second and third stunning transfigurations of "Prodigal" come toward the end, when the young girl hurting herself turns into words herself, taking the scissors "to that perfect page," and then turns, again, into the very world, into *"her other body"*: the maternal or feminized earth, of which we are all a part, destroying ourselves. The whole world is cutting itself to pieces in its shame. I was simply not prepared for the complexity of this trope. Yet it felt, even on first reading, entirely right. How did this ending come about? Was it early or late in the process of composition when you determined how the poem should terminate?

LG: It was very late. I was stuck for a long, long time. It's always the hardest, and the truest, part of composition for me: reaching a point where the poem needs to go more deeply into itself by going elsewhere. Authentically elsewhere, somewhere I haven't pre-plotted. I often find that point by writing slightly beyond it, into a fulfillment that's too predictable. So I have to cut back to the precipice and be stranded there for a while. It's a very uncomfortable place; it drives me crazy. And it's where the thing either does or does not become a poem.

DB: Let's set aside, for now, the issue of subject matter, but let's talk some more about how something becomes a poem. Readers of your work—those many of us who've followed your poetry especially since *The Woman Who Died in Her Sleep* in 1996—are likely to be fascinated by these two poems, as by nearly all the poems in your new book, *Magnetic North,* for their adventurous ranging-out into more formal variety. In your last two books you developed and perfected a sinuous stanza form, a very flexible, spacious indented triad stanza.

What did that triad permit you to do, or to explore? And why have you left it to move into further kinds of formal designs? How do all of these formal tactics or practices help your writing, as you say, to become a poem?

LG: That tercet quite flatly saved my life. Before I found it, and I found it simply by playing around with a thousand variants, I had written in "block stanzas," everything flush left, and had become very unhappy indeed with the result. Those rectangular blocks were deeply falsifying, I thought—for me, that is. They were airless; they completely obscured the cadences I'd tried to embody in syntax. The tercets were the first formal vehicle I found that seemed to me to be properly flexible, and true. Especially important was that second, deeply indented line, the "pivot line" as I conceived it, often only a single metrical foot long. It gave me a kind of skeletal resistance, something that syntax could work against, and thus it became a true generative proposition, not just a kind of packaging. The lineation produced the poem.

And as with any codependency, it got to be too much. I began to worry that I knew that stanza too well, knew not only the music but the shape of the cognitive or affective discoveries it tended to incite. So I've tried to experiment again.

DB: In all of your poems, the sinuous form and stanza permits you a kind of play. There must be a formal corollary between the concrete artifact of your style and the rigor or method of thinking itself. Your sentences and lines unwind, unpack, ravel and unravel, in and out. This feels like a mind at work, musing, pressing. How do you decide on a poem's form, especially in *Magnetic North,* where there are so many different technical strategies—strategies of line, syntax, stanza? At what point in the composing do you settle on shape?

LG: I have to decide very early; I simply can't write the poem without a provisional shape for the stanza. So I locate the early phrasing, the language with which the poem is to begin, and try to "score" it against (that's a telling confession, no doubt: against) a pattern of lineation. And I throw it out and start again—it has to be on the computer by now—and fiddle with it endlessly until I have something I think will accommodate the pitch of diction, the relative pacing, the formality or informality of the voicing. Line five never, ever gets written until lines three and four are firmly in place.

The first poem I wrote for this new book, the poem called "Elegant," is all over the page; I expect the excessive ranginess was part of a not-too-subtle effort to convince myself there was life after the tercet. But it also felt, and feels to me, that the form is somehow suited to the subject, to that blessed little roundworm, *C. elegans,* and the remarkable story of its embryonic cell lineage. I had in mind a particular graphic—the breakthrough paper that mapped the thousand-and-ninety cells of the embryo and the divisions that produce them was accompanied, in the pages of *Developmental Biology,* by a twelve-page chart: it looks like a kind of musical score. But I also had in mind the movement of hypothesis and revision that is so beautiful a part of scientific method.

Most of the new poems are more obedient formally: they have a more predictable relationship to the left-hand margin. Though obedience is a relative thing: I am so wedded to asymmetry, it is to me so necessary and native a vocal element, that working in couplets feels wild.

DB: Asymmetry, yes, I see that. Your rhetorical argument and your technical form both tend to unspool, and wind around, and go-in-search-of. But I also note the formality of your method of closure. I guess it's not exactly symmetrical closure, but certainly and frequently a kind of dignity or classical enclosing. I feel quite the opposite, at the end of your poems, than I do at the ending of other poets' scattered or asymmetrical lyrics. I mean, about your endings, the frequency of a final line or phrasing in perfect iambic 0 tetrameter or pentameter. Or your occasional sly internal rhyme at the end. The poems often snap shut like a Shakespearean sonnet.

As I scan through *Magnetic North,* I count only four poems of the book's eighteen that do *not* end in a long iambic phrase. Now the iamb is the normative rhythm throughout your poems, but often very loosely so. These endings, though, really formalize the iambic phrase and serve as a remarkable closing gesture. "And then she blows the candle out," finishes one. "I think I'll call this mercy too"; "It's wholly premise, rather like the crusted snow"; and even "Elegant" with its "excessive ranginess," as you rightly call it, concludes with "this thread of in-the-cells remembering made it so."

LG: My cover blown! But you're entirely right, of course, and "classical" is the generous way to put it. I work inside a tightly bounded metric; it's all I can do to vary the pattern with dactyls and anapests or to end a clause on an unstressed syllable. That's one of the reasons syntax is so important to me: if the syntactical units expand and contract, if they can be made to move with variable pressure, then there's something at odds with the meter.

DB: Sure, that makes sense, the way the syntax can assist in varying the meter. Your line breaks, too, the uneven procedure of the form, the indentions—all those tactical aspects are part of the poem's internal argument with the regularity of its rhythm.

LG: Yes, thank you, that puts it very clearly.

DB: Let's talk more about *Magnetic North.* The book delights me for its range (of subject matter and formal architecture, as we are exploring) as well as for its lyrical beauty. You are working at your height. How do you write books? A poem at a time? Or do you conceive of a book's identity early on? How did you put this collection together?

LG: I'm sure if I were a better person I would work more conceptually earlier on, but in fact it tends to be poem by poem at first. And then, if I'm lucky, the poems begin to talk to one another, and I begin to think of a larger arc, and then the last part—the half or third at the end—is written *into* the larger shape or trajectory.

DB: You mean that some of the final poems come along to you with a fairly clear place in the book? Or that you sense the kind of thing you want a late-written poem to do, in its relationship to the other extant poems?

LG: It's usually a question of proportion, as in, "another splotch of yellow in the lower left, please." One of the last poems I completed for *Magnetic*

North was the quasi-title poem, "*De Magnete*." In that case, there was a very clear place the poem was required to fill, but it was a conceptual place, not a slot in the sequence.

DB: Can you say what that conceptual place—that idea—was at the time, before you wrote the poem? Did it feel like a gap of some sort? That's a fascinating kind of awareness.

LG: As I mentioned, the first poem I completed for this volume was a long poem, "Elegant," which takes as its subject the investigations of three physiologists, John Sulston, Robert Horvitz, and Sydney Brenner, who happen to have won the Nobel Prize in Physiology in 2002. I'd located my title—*Magnetic North*—perhaps a third of the way into the writing of the book. After some missteps, I'd finally located the cover art: a beautiful white-on-white construction by the German artist Günther Uecker. This painting—it is a painting of sorts—consists of hundreds and hundreds of nails pounded into a wooden panel, the whole of it painted white, and the nails projecting two inches or so from the front of the panel. So that the *real* painting consists of shadows and light: the myriad shadows cast by these little white poles, shadows which seem to organize themselves in patterns but patterns that alter completely when the light source alters. The links among all these elements—the little roundworm and its cell divisions, the microscopy that gives us access to them, the magnetic pole and its ties to navigation, the love letter (scientific and painterly) to partial views, the critique of partial views, the cold beauty of a world that only tenuously aligns with our ability to construe it—these links were vivid in my mind but largely implicit in the manuscript. I needed something with a more explicit link to the title of the book especially. A horrifying baggy monster of motives. So I started reading: about the history of navigation, polar exploration, the search for the magnetic north pole, the general science of magnetism. And when I came to William Gilbert and *De Magnete*—he published that book in 1600!—I finally had something that, I hoped, could touch the chords I needed to touch without getting hopelessly tangled in them. That unit of the personal—one man's biography, one man's evolving method, one man's curiosity—can be hopelessly sentimentalizing and simplistic, of course, but simplifying units are also very powerful; they give us a through-line; they're hospitable; I've learned not to scorn them.

DB: What do you want this particular book to do for its readers? It will have readers, I am certain of that.

LG: I hope the poems catch something of our common grief for the world as we've harmed it, and our common gratitude for all the goodness we haven't yet managed to expunge. I hope—I feel like Blanche DuBois, relying upon the kindness of strangers—I hope the patient reader will find, in the quarrel between velocity and stumble, woven surface and fissure or tear, some fleeting approximation of the present tense. I hope—it's outrageous to hope this, but every writer does, I think—I hope the poems, or some piece of them somewhere, even for a tiny bit, can stall the rush to oblivion.

DB: I learn things when I read your poems and your books. I wish that were true more often of the poetry I read. Poetry is not information, to be sure. As Daniel Tiffany reminds us, "Only a fool reads poetry for facts." Yet poetry can contain and pass along knowledge, wisdom, as well as song and the processes of thinking. You seem pretty fearless in your thinking, in the ways your poems include historical data and narratives, medical treatments, specific scientific information, to say nothing of your recreations of theatrical performances and art installations. I tend to think of your work as more inclusive than not, more impure than pure. Is that a fair depiction?

LG: The world is so rich with the cumulative textures of material practice, the intricate dynamics of our own and other people's daily labors, the tenuous workings of human memory—it seems a pity if poetry is to leave them out.

DB: Then what is the relationship, in lyric poetry, between purity and the impure? Or is that a misleading dichotomy from the start?

LG: Certainly there are poets who work on what seems to us the purer end of the spectrum: those for whom the distillations of personal experience and lyric tradition or the rigors of philosophical meditation constitute a durable and continuous medium. For the rest of us, those who treasure the disruptions and "contaminants," the poem has to justify its existence in other ways. What keeps the poem from being merely secondary or after-the-fact? Ekphrastic poetry has a long and honorable history, but I think it should always be uneasy on this ground. The neurophysiologists whose work I all but worship don't need my little lyric after all. But I do think the world needs more of neurophysiology (and history, and equine dentistry, for that matter) than its practitioners and professional explicators are in the habit of providing (they have their own good work to do). I think there are rhythms of thought, fragile propositions about the intersections of human understanding and human habitus, robust intersections of the pragmatic and the sublime, that science shares with art, and I love the thought that poetry can learn from and do homage to its near cousins. The great thing about "facts" (and the scientists are much more sophisticated skeptics than the poets are) is that they put up resistance. Resistance is good for art, and for thinking in general.

DB: You have worked as a teacher for a long time. Your permanent position is at the University of Michigan. What are the specifics of your position there? What do you teach?

LG: My scholarly training is in Renaissance literature, and Michigan has always been wonderful about allowing me to teach an array of courses in that field as well as courses in creative writing. At present, I'm teaching a graduate course with a colleague in the history department on "Religion and Empire in the Early Modern Atlantic" and also an undergraduate course on lyric poetry.

DB: I'm not even going to ask the obvious question, which is how you manage to balance your teaching and your teaching and your writing and all your other familial and professional commitments. Still, I know you also are generous in your willingness to teach elsewhere—at the Bread Loaf Writers' Conference, for instance, or the Warren Wilson M.F.A. program for writers, or at our own *Kenyon Review* summer workshop. How do you find the time? Can you explain why people seem to be turning in substantial numbers to these kinds of opportunities to study and to write poetry?

LG: I adore teaching at Bread Loaf and Kenyon and the Warren Wilson residencies; their intensity always astonishes and invigorates me. It's quite remarkable to put aside everything else for a week or two and immerse oneself in the written word and a community of people who care so deeply for it. Writing itself is generally solitary; Judith Grossman once wonderfully described the process as a chronic "social insult." So one hungers for a kind of antidote, I think: some form of being-alone-in-company, or frankly taking a break from aloneness. Pragmatically, of course, many writers spend their working days in other pursuits, and the chance to receive intensive feedback on manuscripts, to share ideas and strategies and reading lists, is invaluable.

DB: At Michigan you come into close contact with some of the finest young poets in the country. It's an impressive program, personal in its size and kind of contact. What are the students like these days? Can you characterize their writing, their reading, their interests? If it's possible to summarize a new generation of poets, what might be some of their strengths and weaknesses?

LG: The students are wonderfully varied in their methods and aesthetics. Some are working on a shattered page, in fragmentary syntax, with conspicuous debts to contemporary music and visual culture. Some are working in a much more restrained and classical vein. Many of them have decided to test the parameters of their own "found forms" by writing from time to time in a received or inherited form, even in rhyme. One is working on a Pushkin-style novel-in-verse. Several are experimenting with performance modes or collaborations with visual artists, videographers, musicians. Many poets now, not just the young but especially the young, are compelled by mixed genres. The possibilities are terribly exciting.

The challenge, predictably enough, lies in tempering all this burgeoning possibility with some meaningful form of stricture. One wants the gorgeous, expanded palette of color and movement but one doesn't want to be a perpetual dilettante. The expansion of methods must somehow lead to freshening or intensification rather than a watering-down. The problem is daunting and thrilling at once: how to locate the hard edge, the limits, the embodied grammar that will give this new work its own center of gravity.

DB: How does one teach someone else to be a poet?

LG: I suppose one teaches everything but that. I try to encourage in my students a meticulous attention to the elements of poetry: to syntax, image, idiom, cognitive pacing, tone. To punctuation, for heaven's sake. I try to teach them to be wary of paraphrase: to hunt down and banish all those poetry-impersonators we all let into our work from time to time, those moments of reporting-on-discoveries-made-elsewhere. I try to encourage them to think on the page. The real poets are those who make use of it all: they hone their craft to accommodate a single, foundational motive, a sort of cognitive hunger. Mindfulness, you might call it, or good faith curiosity.

DB: Linda, one of the other primary forms of your own curiosity involves the theater. You were an actor some time ago, and for years, in Herbert Blau's company Kraken. Many of your poems find their narrative centers literally inside a play. I think of an older poem like "Target," with its juxtaposition of Medea and the crisis in Serbia or of "A History Play." "Eyes Like Leeks" follows Thisby from *A Midsummer Night's Dream*, the selfsame Thisby who recurs in your new poem "No Lion, No Moon." In fact, your new book features a number of dramatic scenes and tropes—from plays old and new.

LG: The theater taught me how to think. That is, it taught me about embodied thinking. So it was and is foundational. And the play-within-a-play in *Midsummer Night's Dream*! Right up there with the Book of Genesis!

DB: Even beyond your literal application of dramatic works, the stance or position of the voice of your poems sometimes feels projected in something of the way I imagine an actor's persona must be impelled and clarified. It has to do with articulation, I think, and projection. How do you think about the relation of the theater or performance in the sphere of the lyric poem, with its typical meditative or unvoiced voice?

LG: An actor discovers where to go by going there; she begins with a gesture and then it fills. The ones that fail to fill, you scuttle. In other words, the process is pure induction. It becomes a kind of sense-memory, and I find it a useful antidote to the ways in which "emotion recollected in tranquility" can lapse into paraphrase. We all wash up on this phenomenon from time to time, I think: one may begin with intensest feeling, but if the poem chiefly reports on intensities discovered off the page, the poem remains forever secondary. The lyric poem has to be at risk in the present tense; actors, alas, know all about this.

DB: Your other academic life is as a Renaissance scholar. Your book, *The Reformation of the Subject,* examines the early modern epic—both Spenser's and Milton's. And other recent critical work looks at Isabella Whitney, among others. What again might you say about the application of your scholarly period to your poetry? Or vice versa? Your poems seem so, well, contemporary. Do you think about, or even engineer, some kinds of overlap? Do you exploit any kinds of difference? I'm thinking beyond the occasional allusion and reference to the Renaissance in your poems.

LG: This brings us back to your previous question, actually, about voicing in the lyric poem. I'm increasingly convinced that this was the great contribution of the sixteenth-century English lyricists, Wyatt especially, which we see coming to such remarkable fruition some eighty years later, in Marvell, Shakespeare, Donne: they experimented with quasi-dramatic gestures of voicing as though these were another kind of trope. *Quasi*-dramatic: quite separate from the evolution of the Renaissance stage or those later consolidations we call dramatic monologue. Wyatt simply does not sustain a continuous meditative fabric: he allows the lyric surface to be disrupted by the symptoms of personality. He devises the lyric "self" as a kind of intermittent back-formation. He opens up this wonderful, porous rhetoricity, a perpetually shifting contract of expectation between speaker and auditor. I don't—I couldn't possibly—mimic any of it directly, but I do find analogies in the fabric of contemporary American poetry, an effort to push the extra-referential aspects of language toward a kind of performativity.

DB: I am really pleased to thank you here for another variety of your scholarly work—that is, for your participation in a new book I have coedited, with Ann Townsend. *Radiant Lyre: Essays on Lyric Poetry* has just been released by Graywolf, and of course you know how proud and grateful we are to feature five new essays of yours in this book, a study of some of the fundamental modes of the lyric poem. You have written on the ode, the love poem, the sublime, and the problems of time and of people in the lyric genre.

LG: *Radiant Lyre* is a great joy to me because of the way in which it emerged: as a kind of public conversation among people who care deeply about the practice and the history of lyric. That engaged conversation is exactly what criticism is at heart.

DB: I agree. An engaged conversation is the essence of criticism. It is also—in a different way—the essence of poetry. We tend to regard the lyric poem as a personal, even private utterance. But in *Radiant Lyre,* your essay "Life among Others" speaks very persuasively of the social engagement, the social identity, of the lyric. As you say, "The lyric poem is a form of social speaking. . . . It *emerges* as singular in the process of social encounter and social thinking-through." I take it that social encounter and thinking-through are not merely references to narrative—or to poems with people in dramatic circumstances—but also to poetic form and troping themselves. Is that what you mean? The contours and references, the very substance of a poem are embedded in our social memory and our social exchanges. The self is part of that social fabric.

LG: Yes, indeed: poetic form, like language itself, is a rich and sedimented legacy. We don't make it up from scratch. We may seek to expand or alter the range of possibilities, but we never work outside the basic social fact. There's a theoretical crux at stake here too: I'm among the many people who found it terribly exciting when post-structuralism encouraged us to be skeptical about the post-Enlightenment valorization of the individual. Writers in a number of disciplines began to debunk the notion of an intact inward essence that was ontologically if not temporally prior to culture; they began to speak about the self, or subjectivity, as an effect rather than a premise. It was all rather exhilarating, and of course there was a serious political critique at stake as well. And, as is wont to be the case with All the New Thinking in any of its guises, the insight was largely a revival of an older understanding. Poetry has always known that the subject is a made thing: made by longing for another, made by sorrow and the friction of daily getting-on-with-it, made above all by speech.

DB: Poet, critic, teacher, reader, scholar. You are many things. What do you see happening in poetry right now? Emerson says the genius is someone who can see today. What can you see? What is not happening in our poetry that, perhaps, should be?

LG: On the one hand, I'm quite heartened by the sheer plenitude of contemporary American poetry, its formal and cultural and methodological range. Performativity is at the heart of it, I think—just a minute ago, I called that quality "extra-referential," but perhaps I'd do better to call it *compounded* reference. So much of the most interesting poetry at present involves an aggravated tension among the various motives and allegiances of language: words as serviceable instruments, words as social glue, words as symptoms, words as smoke screen, words as sympathetic magic. I'm thrilled to see how many poets seem to care about history again, how capaciously the lyric poem is being used to expand our range not just of cultural reference but of cultural *recognition*. In the beautiful elegy for his mother, "From Amherst to Kashmir," Agha Shahid Ali finds a way to create for all his readers a site of common mourning, a kind of psychic home—and this in the vocabularies of Shiite Islam.

That said, I think we still, we Americans, suffer from underdevelopment when it comes to poetry and the contested, large-scale differentials of power we often refer to as "politics." Poets are dreadfully behind the writers of fiction in this regard, more so than the varying aptitudes of literary genre would require. We're desperately afraid of moral earnestness. But why should that be the reigning specter? We need somehow to enlarge and deepen the terms of engagement.

DB: Yes, we do, Linda. And that is what I think your poetry succeeds in doing for us all.

Fady Joudah

SALEH SOUBRA

FADY JOUDAH was born on New Year's Day in 1971 in Austin, Texas, to Palestinian refugee parents. He grew up in Libya and Saudi Arabia, speaking Arabic as his first language. After receiving an undergraduate degree in microbiology at the University of Georgia, he went on for his medical degree at the Medical College of Georgia and subsequently received training at the University of Texas in Houston, in internal medicine, where he served as chief medical resident. Later he served as an emergency room physician in the Veterans Hospital in Houston for eight years. Currently he works in clinics in the Houston area; he has also traveled twice, to Darfur and to Zambia, with the humanitarian organization Doctors Without Borders. Joudah's wife, Hana, is a physician at the Baylor Medical College, specializing in infectious diseases. They have a one-year-old son, Ziyad. Hana's daughter, Mona, completes their family of four.

Joudah's poetry is rich with the influences and styles of both American and Arabic poetry. It can be personal and image driven, by turns, as well as discursive and social. Its lyric gifts are as powerful as its narrative impulse. Though he has said that political poetry is often "propagandist or apologist for injustice," Joudah's work is notable for its cultural conscience as well as its commitment to a sense of justice. His poems and translations have appeared widely in the past few years, including in *The New Yorker* and *Poetry*.

Fady Joudah won the 2007 Yale Series of Younger Poets Prize for his first collection of poems, *The Earth in the Attic,* published in 2008 by Yale University Press. The award was judged by Louise Glück, who wrote that "the book is varied, coherent, fierce, tender: impossible to put down, impossible to forget." Joudah's translation of Mahmoud Darwish's *The Butterfly's Burden* appeared in 2007 from Copper Canyon Press and has been widely and enthusiastically reviewed. The translation was shortlisted for the PEN award for poetry in translation, and received the Saif Ghobash-Banipal prize for Arabic translation from the UK's Society of Authors, in 2008. His new translation of Darwish's poetry, *If I Were Another,* appeared from Farrar Straus & Giroux in 2010.

Still Life

You write your name on unstained glass
So you're either broken or seen through

When it came time for the affidavit
The panel asked how much art
Over the blood of strangers the word

Mentioned the weather and the sleepers
Under the weather all this
Was preceded by tension enzymatic
To the hills behind us and the forests ahead

Where children don't sleep
In resting tremor and shelling
The earth is a pomegranate

A helmet ochre or copper sinks
In buoyant salt water
Divers seek its womb despite its
Dura mater

And it hangs on trees like pregnant mistletoes
I'll stand next to one and have my German lover

Remember me on a Mediterranean island
Though she would eventually wed
An Israeli once she'd realized
What she wanted from life

A mother of two
On the nose of Mount Carmel
Where my wife's father was born driven out
But there lies the rub O Lord

My father's hands depearl
The fruit in a few minutes add a drop

Of rose water some shredded coconut
For us to gather around him

He will lead his grandchildren out transfer
Bundles of pine branches in the yard to where
His tomatoes and cucumbers grow in summer

Let them let them
Gather the dried pine needles forever he says
They will refuse to believe the fire dies

And they will listen to his first fire
On a cold night in a forest of eucalyptus trees
The British had planted as natural reserve
Outside Gaza

Smoke

With a cigarette in her left hand she says love built the gazebo . . .
Thirty years after the smoke between the two clans had cleared

His from a village meaning Little Planet
In the costal plains hers from the city of golden locks

They were off to a faraway country of immigrants
No blood was shed no wedding only marriage

Then her husband sought identity in manuscripts
At the oldest campus on another continent

There were riots there the philosophers had joined the students
Fumes arched and landed into the cuff of his pants

It had been the first time he'd seen teargas
Bombs even though he was among those who

Decades prior had burned down an ancient capital . . .
He flicked his leg and the bomb went flying into the crowd

He's next to her now
Her second hand smoke

Even if he was once caught in a street battle during a civil war
He rushed inside the first door

That would open a madam greeted him and offered
One of her girls for a fee and in a second he

Was back out on the street
Said he had scripts to write and scrolls to find . . .

Twice a River

After studying our faces for four months
My son knows to beam is the thing to do

He'll spend years
Deciphering the injustice or the illusion of it

Which depends on love
Having been brought into this world

Volition is an afterthought

What will I tell him
About land and language and burial

Places my father doesn't speak of

Perhaps my mother knows
In the movie the dispossessed cannot return

Even when they're dead
The journalist felt

Rebuke for not having thought
It mattered or for having thought it mattered too much

Will I
Tell my son all nations arise after mass

Murder—that I don't know

Any national anthem by heart can't sing
Before or after games or between innings?

I should turn to flowers and clouds instead
Though this has already been said well

It is night when he gazes
Into his mother's eyes at bath time

Qyss and Laila she announces after a long day's work

He giggles with his shoulders not knowing
He's installing a web

In his amygdala or whichever
Places science thinks love dwells

For the future—even love is a place? O son

Love no country and hate none
And remember crimes sometimes

Immortalize their victims
Other times the victimizer

Remember how you used to gaze at the leaves
The breeze on trampoline branches?

Don't believe the sound of the sea
In a seashell—believe the sea

The endless trope and don't say
Much about another's language

If you don't speak it well
Learn to love it

While observing silence
For the dead and the living in it

POEMS BY MAHMOUD DARWISH

If I Were Another

In solitude lies the competency of one entrusted with himself—he writes a phrase, looks up at the ceiling, then adds: To be alone . . . to be able to be alone is self-taught. Solitude is a selection of pain brands, and an exercise, of a free sovereign self, in conjugating the verbs of the heart . . . or it is what resembles one's lack of his exterior, and an emergency landing in one's self without a parachute . . . Alone you sit, like an idea in no need of proof's apparent and the concealed. Solitude is a filter, not a mirror. You toss what's in your left hand over to your right one, and nothing changes in this relocation from non-idea to non-meaning. Yet this innocent frivolity is harmless and fruitless: So what if I am alone? Solitude is the choosing of what is profligate with the probable . . . a choosing of what's free. So when you dry up and are fed up with yourself, you say: If I were another I would leave this white paper and converse with a Japanese novel whose author climbs to the mountaintop to see what predator birds have done with his ancestors. Perhaps he is still writing, and his dead are still dying. But I lack the experience, and the metaphysical harshness. If I were another, as I am now, I would walk down to the belly of the wadi, where a young woman is kindling her suppressed libido with a coarse fig leaf as she holds her dress in her mouth, but I lack the descriptive talent. And the licentious audacity.

Rustle

And like one who listens to a hidden revelation, I listen to the summer leaves . . . a timid, anesthetized sound, descending from the distances of sleep . . . a pale sound with a wheat scent coming from a rural seclusion . . . intermittent, composed, improvised on the strings of a serene breeze. It neither runs on nor prolongs its musical segments. The sound of summer leaves have the ascetics of whispers and the austerity of calling. As if this sound is mine alone, it kidnaps me from the heaviness of substance to the lightness of radiance: There behind the hills, and beyond the imagination, where the apparent and the concealed are equal, I swim outside my self in a sunless light. And after a nap that resembles wakefulness, or a wakefulness that resembles a nap, the rustle of leaves brings me back safe and sound, sorted out of apprehensions and obsessions. I don't ask about the meaning of the sound: Is it a soliloquy between two sister leaves, or the air's longing to a siesta? A speechless sound dandles me, messages me and turns me into a vessel that exudes what isn't or it or in it . . . as if it were a sentiment searching for a sentimental look alike.

At a Train Station That Fell Off the Map

Grass, dry air, thorns, and cactus
on the iron wire. There's the shape of a thing
in the frivolity of non shape chewing its shadow . . .
a bound void . . . encircled up by its opposite.
And there are two doves hovering
over the roof of an abandoned room at the station
and the station is a tattoo that has melted
In the body of place. There are also two
slim cypresses like two long needles
that embroider a lemon-yellow cloud,
and a tourist woman taking photos of two scenes:
a sun that has stretched in the sea's bed
and a wooden bench that is vacant of the traveler's sac

(The hypocrite heavenly gold is bored with its own solidity)

I stood at the station, not to wait for the train
or for emotions hidden in the aesthetics of some faraway thing,
but to know how the sea went mad and the place broke
like a ceramic jar, to know where I was born and how I lived,
and how the birds migrated to the north and south.
Is what remains of me enough
for the weightless imaginary to triumph
over the corruption of fact?
Is my gazelle still pregnant?

(We have aged. O how we've aged, and the road to the sky is long)

The train used to travel like a friendly snake from Syria
through Egypt. Its whistle concealed
the husky bleats of goats from the wolves' hunger.
As if it were a mythical time that tamed wolves to befriend us.
Its smoke used to rise over the smoke of villages
which opened up and appeared like shrubs in nature.

(Life is intuitive. Our homes and hearts have open doors)

We were kindhearted and naïve. We said: The land is our land
and no external affliction will befall the map's heart.
And the sky is generous to us. We hardly spoke to each other
in classical Arabic, save at prayer time and on holy nights.
Our present serenaded us: Together we live!
Our past amused us: I'll come back if you need me!
We were kindhearted and dreamy, we didn't see
tomorrow steal the past, his prey, and leave . . .

(A while ago our present used to grow wheat and squash and make the
        wadi dance)

I stood at the station at sunset: Are there still two women
in one woman who is polishing her thigh with lightening?
Two mythic-enemy-friends and twins
on the surface of wind, one who flirts with me, and another
who wars with me? Has spilled blood ever broken
a single sword, so I can say my first Goddess is still within me?

(I believed my old song so I can disbelieve my reality)

The train was a land ship docking . . . it carried us to the realistic
cities of our imagination whenever we were in need
of innocent play with destiny. Train windows possess
the magical in the ordinary: everything runs.
Trees, ideas, waves, towers run
behind us. And the lemon scent runs. The air and the rest
of things run, and the longing
to a mysterious faraway, and the heart, run.

(Everything differed and agreed)

I stood at the station, I was as abandoned as the timekeeper's
room there. I was a dispossessed man staring
at his closet and asking himself: Was that
mind, that treasure, mine? Was this
damp lapis lazuli, humidity and nightly dew, mine?

Was I one day the butterfly's pupil
in fragility, and in audacity, and was I her mate
in metaphor at times? Was one of those days
mine? Or does memory fall ill also and catch a fever?

(I see my trace on a stone, I think it's my moon, and chant)

Another ruin and I'll snuff my memories while standing
at the station. I don't love this grass now, this
forgotten aridity, frivolous and desolate
it writes the biography of forgetting in this mercurial place.
And I don't love chrysanthemum over the tombs of prophets.
And I don't love rescuing my self through metaphor, even if
the violin wants me as an echo of my self. I only love return
to my life, for my end to become my beginning's narrative.

(Like the clang of bells, time broke here)

I stood in the sixtieth year of my wound. I stood
at the station, not to await the train or the holler
of those who return from the south to the grains
but to memorize the olive and lemon coast
in my map's history . . . is all
this absence or what remains of its crumbs mine?
Did a ghost pass me by, wave from afar and disappear?
Did I ask him: Will we slaughter a gazelle
for the stranger whenever a stranger
smiles to us and casts us a greeting?

(Like a pinecone echo fell from me)

Only my intuition guides me to my self.
Two fugitive doves lay exile's eggs on my shoulder
then soar to a pale height. A tourist woman passes by
and asks me: Can I take your picture to respect the truth?
I said: What do you mean?
She said: Can I take your picture
as an extension of nature? I said: You can . . . everything
is possible, and have a great evening and leave me alone
with dying . . . and with my self

(Here truth has one single lonely face and that's why I'll sing)

You are you, even if you lose. In the past
you and I are two, and in tomorrow, one. The train passed
but we weren't alert, so rise up complete and optimistic,
and wait for no one here, beside yourself. Here the train fell
off the map in the middle of the coastal path. And the fires
flamed in the heart of the map, then winter
extinguished the fires, though winter was late.
We have aged, O how we've aged before we could return
to our first names:

(I say to whoever sees me through the binoculars on the watchtower I
        don't see you . . . I don't see you)

I see all of my place around me. I see me in the place with all
my limbs and organs. I see palm trees edit my classical
Arabic from error. I see almond blossoms,
their habits in training my song for a sudden
joy. I see my trace and follow it. I see my shadow
and lift it from the wadi with a bereaved Canaanite
woman's comb. I see what cannot be seen of attractive
flow and whole beauty in the eternity
of the hills, and don't see my snipers.

(I become my self's guest)

There are dead who light fires around their graves.
There are living who prepare dinner for their guests.
There are enough words for metaphor to rise
above incident. Whenever the place dims a copper moon
illuminates and expands it. I am my self's guest.
A hospitality that will embarrass and delight me, until I choke
on words and words choke on obstinate tears . . . and the dead,
along with the living, drink immortality's mint, without
talking much about Resurrection Day

(There's no train there, and no one will wait for the train)

Our country is the map's heart. Its punctured heart
like a coin in the metal market. The last passenger from somewhere
between Syria and Egypt didn't return to pay the fee
for some extra work the sniper did . . . as the strangers expected.
The last passenger didn't return and didn't carry his death
and life certificates along, for the sages of Judgment Day to discern
his place in Paradise. O we were angels and fools
when we believed the banners and the horses
and that a falcon's wing will raise us up high

(My sky is an idea, and the earth is my favorite exile)

All there is to it is that I only believe my intuition.
Evidence conducts the dialogue of the impossible. The story
of creation belongs to the philosopher's long-winded interpretation.
My idea about the world has a malfunction
departure has caused. My eternal wound stands trial
without an impartial judge. And the judges, exhausted
by truth, tell me: All there is to it is that
traffic accidents are common: the train fell off the map
and you burned with the ember of the past: this
wasn't an invasion . . .

but I say: All there is to it is that
I only believe my intuition

(I'm still alive)

Past the Centrality
of Suffering

A Conversation with Fady Joudah

David Baker: Fady, thank you for finding time in your packed schedule to talk about your work and life. I am happy to talk here about some of your new poems along with a few of your recent translations of Mahmoud Darwish's work. American readers have come to know Darwish only lately, thanks in part to your advocacy and translation. What did his death last year mean to you, and to other poets in the Arabic world and language?

Fady Joudah: I am not sure I can fully grasp what his death means to me or to others. I think in one manner it affords me that invaluable experience of speaking with the dead, as it were, through my working and reworking of language in my own poems. There is an endless well in Darwish's aesthetics, private and universal, original and communal, with which one can correspond and journey. And you are right, this depth has only begun to be searched and embraced only recently in English.

On a larger scale, however, I think Arab poetry and poets are now in a moment that is no longer dominated by the giant figures (of Adonis, Saadi Yussef, Darwish, et cetera). I think Darwish's death brings a particular era of innovation to a close and opens up to unknown possibilities in aesthetics and form. For example, the endless debate over the form of the contemporary Arab poem, between prosody and prose, free taf'eelah (the basic unit of prosody) and free verse, has now entered a wider dimension of experimentation. Darwish was an amazing innovative formalist who refused to simply accept that one school of poetry negates another. He believed that contemporary Arabic is easily able to embrace its modern moment, away from the nebulae of colloquial versus classical Arabic, which is sometimes brought up in English when discussing Arabic (by many who do not speak it well). Darwish touches on this issue in "Train Station" but with a "native's eye" toward the end of the poem, when he mentions how classical Arabic was spoken only in formal, literate social gatherings.

DB: I'd like to talk a lot more about Darwish and his poetry, as well as your work as a translator from the Arabic. I also have some related questions for you about recent Arabic poetry and prosody and what you call the modern moment. So let's come back around to those things by looking at your own poems, especially this group in the new *Kenyon Review*. Are they from a new collection, or manuscript, or are you working one poem at a time just now?

FJ: Yes, these poems are part of a new manuscript titled *Alight*. They are in its second half. The life of family and parenthood as it relates to the mind in the world. The manuscript continues the dialogue with art as it appropriates the suffering of others, which is not a problem specific to art, obviously. Politics and power engage in this, albeit to a much more horrific extent. In part I feel it is the age-old question of the imbalance between memory and forgetfulness, testimony and complicity. It is a slippery slope, however, when this art is essentially an art of empire.

DB: *Alight* is a great title. It also is a good example of the kind of thing I find so powerful, and sometimes playful, in your work. That is, the doubling of meanings. To alight is to land, as a bird does on a limb or a reader on an image. It means to brighten, to shine on; and it also suggests a kind of levity or lightness. But it also sounds like something has been set on fire, a fuse, a bomb, a pyre.

This is the fundamental method of your work, to me, the way your images deepen into metaphor, the way the metaphors often measure the particular with the general, and the way they argue with each other. You seem at home with contradictions. As you just said, testimony and complicity.

FJ: *Alight* starts a flame and sets the inflammatory against the humane, before the fire turns gradually into light and alights onto the familial discourse of love and its contradictions, its insolvable difficulties at times, through the experience of fatherhood and husbandry.

Images for me are an ancient trope, if one may say that, of poetry. I grew up to the idea of metaphorical conceit borne out of weaving images and emotional being, in Arabic poetry, and not necessarily as direct influence of the twentieth-century school. That the ancient and the new, the foreign and the domestic intersect is evidence of the universality of the language of poetry in the human mind. Neuroscience argues well for this. Still, Arabic romanticism exists independently of (and much earlier than) its Western kin. Maybe it wasn't a movement per se, but Arabic romanticism has been present and developing for a thousand years.

As for the particular and the general, I also think this is an ancient poetic trope: the balance of the private and the universal, the personal and the collective. Yet in our modern times, and because of my predilection for engaging life in the administered world in which we live, I am (hyper)vigilant of the darkness that moral certainty can bring into poetry; it can bring poetry to its knees, damage the art and the artist. The contradiction is not a wily maneuver to remain elusive and to "read between the lines," however. It is an attempt to universalize the particulars of tragedy and suffering, of humanity, that of the speaker and of the "other." I struggle with and against the classification of suffering, which often perpetuates further dehumanization of victims, through justification of violence or of silence.

DB: Yes, you mentioned earlier the slippery slope of art and empire. Empire, or empires, is the subject of your poem "Smoke." I love the hybrid quality of this poem. It is a portrait of two people—though they remain anonymous—but it is also cultural and political commentary. Warfare and love. Philosophy and a sex shop. Many things here are alit with clarity and contradiction.

Louise Glück noted that your poems, your images, often seem like analogues for photographs. There's something distinctly photographic about this poem, as it captures real detail in a kind of suspended moment. But inside that moment there is also a very dynamic circumstance. Time passing and time held still.

FJ: Time must be master and subject in a poem. Poetry is, in one manner, the words as they elude and allude to time.

As for the photographic moment, that brings to mind Walter Benjamin's infamous work, *The Work of Art in the Age of Its Technological Reducibility,* about art in the era of cinema. Another way to say it perhaps is through the dynamic of the psychological portrait, which is not without its problems since, like cinema and photography, it lends itself to the troubles of representation and appropriation of the "other." I have been interested recently in the comeback of the historical poem in American poetry, and how it reflects the documentary mode. This really brings the brilliance of Benjamin's prescience to light more.

DB: Susan Sontag's great book *Regarding the Pain of Others* also comes to mind here. She argues that sincerity is what may turn our spectator stance into the stance and responsibility of a witness. Sincerity is here a version, I think, of sympathy. And also, as you say, of historical or social engagement.

I'm delighted by the sympathetic and synthetic language of "Smoke." The poem clarifies its circumstances through its word choice, but then immediately baffles that clarity. For instance, a gazebo is noted in ancient Asian landscapes but also in Persian ones. One etymologist argues that it derives from "casbah," the Muslim quarter in Algiers, but most agree that its origin is, as they say, "unknown." We have here also unnamed ancient capitals alongside teargas, a "faraway country of immigrants," and so on. Specifics and the unknown. Where is this scene?

The poem also feels distinctly multicultural even though it is grounded in a particular place. It even provides its own translations. The village that means Little Planet. All those ancient manuscripts and scrolls.

FJ: Gazebo and similar rootless words are fantastic, aren't they? When you mention "casbah" I immediately flashback to The Clash and their song "Rock the Casbah," and its video on MTV, and how I was always disturbed by its accepted racial representation of the Arab, which is still an accepted situation today in America. Then there is The Cure's "Killing an Arab," which puts us squarely in Edward Said's critique of Albert Camus's absenting of the native in Algeria. Have you read Camus's *The Myth of Sisyphus and Other Essays?* Here is this fantastic existential philosophy at work. Then in the "other essays" he talks of Oran, a major city in Algeria, as if it came without a people. This is obviously not without precedent, and still goes on. So, in "Smoke," why should I name places and get caught up in the jargon of the politics of the day?

DB: Camus's *Sisyphus* was one of those foundational books for me, once upon a time. Are specific names of things jargon? That's an interesting angle. Is the poet's job not, at least in part, to name?

FJ: In Camus's case, it is the absence of naming that is the problem. Paradoxically for me, absence of naming is against the jargon of the classification of suffering, which has become an internationalized décor, it seems, that conveniently tells us which people have suffered more than others and what should be done "about it" (or "for them"), and almost always nothing is done about anything or for anyone except the engraving of moral righteousness in the minds of those who are faraway and watching cable. There is an amazing piece on this by Theodor Adorno, "The Paragraph," contained in his *Minima Moralia.*

DB: Your phrase about the internationalized décor of suffering is really apt but points to the conundrum, too. It speaks to the crux of both Sontag's and Adorno's texts. How do we approach the depth and reality of the genuine suffering and pain of others, without appropriation or without fashioning that pain into the aesthetically palatable?

FJ: There cannot be one specific approach, obviously. I think the speaker in the poems has to know who he is and where he stands in relation to the "other." It is laughably sad to simply substitute pity for compassion. Hannah Arendt has a wonderful essay on this distinction, by the way, "The Social Question." But let's go back to Conrad's *Heart of Darkness* or Kipling's *Kim*. Our (and when I say "our," I mean the citizens of empire) recognition of our own hegemony, or awareness of our tyrannical moral compass, keeps shifting and changing with the passage of historical time. Edward Said's *Culture and Imperialism* is also another important guide to answer this "how" you ask.

DB: Yes, it's partly an issue of awareness in the text, as you say—of conscience.

Back to your poem. Who are the two people? They are trying to live a life of normalcy—whatever that means—in a circumstance of upheaval and destruction. That's even how the title works for me, suggesting both the particular pleasure she derives from her cigarette and the smoke of teargas and bombs.

FJ: It is the seeking of normalcy, the utopian state, which the poem's after, through the humanizing of its protagonists. If I specify things further, then I remove much of the possibility of universalizing the narrative. We are programmed to associate names with Pavlovian responses. It is often a disturbing outcome. Why get sidetracked by excess specificity. Yet we can argue (thankfully) about what defines "excess" or perhaps "extraneous" data, and create different poems that dabble in time. "Smoke" here also is peri-fire. This man's ardent involvement in revolts and manuscripts, truth, fact, and their illusions is just smoke, hot air. He is harmless. Good. Broken. Normal.

DB: The issue of naming is important to "Still Life," also. But you make an important distinction here. The poem opens in the act of writing of the name, but doesn't actually provide the name itself. So I see what you mean about the interplay between the specific and the general. The poem dances back and forth between those two worlds. The poem lives in the space between those two.

FJ: Yet the naming later in the poem is essential, because of its simplicity to me. It is a personal and a familial narrative, not a historic or political one. I also recognize the taboo in it, especially in English. But for me, first and foremost, it is a private narrative: a love affair that engulfs and is consumed by time and history, the linear or otherwise. For example, this poem was written nearly two years ago. Sadly and suddenly the word Gaza takes on a grave and enormous corollary and echo.

DB: The family narrative becomes considerably more personalized in "Twice a River." If the first two poems are more politically driven, this one seems more autobiographical. Yet it is also compelled by its social conscience. The son here "beams" and he "gazes," and while those gestures are lovely in their innocence and simplicity, I also can't help but hear the rhetoric of witness again: the gaze of the viewer or spectator on the familial scene but also on the national and political one. The gaze is not necessarily passive.

Does the gaze ever abate?

FJ: I am not sure I agree the first two poems are more politically driven. When Louise Glück does not identify the characters in her poems (as sister, mother, etc) it does not make her poems less familial or more mythical, for example. "Twice a River" is as political and as familial as the other two are; or is it because it addresses an infant and a young American father that "our" gaze turns toward "our" interiority? Yes, gaze does not abate, it shifts.

Another difficulty the poem addresses is that of the father "passing down" identity to his child. I remember how my sense of self in the world changed after the Israeli invasion of Lebanon in 1982. Now Mona, our daughter, seems obsessed with Gaza, and to tell you the truth we ache over it, her mother and I; we evade her questions about it at times, change the subject.

DB: Your hymn to the son in this poem "O son // Love no country and hate none / And remember crimes sometimes // Immortalize their victims . . ." is part of the multiplicity of your vision, I think. Again, to dance between the worlds of politics and the self, between the Middle East and the West, between the family and the nation, and so on.

I see this as the fundamental, empowering irony of your work. Does that sound accurate to you?

FJ: The multiplicity of my experience deals directly and indirectly with what I believe to be a defining facet of our times: the nation-state (and its harrowing litany of victims, refugees, massacred, dehumanized, and exiles, et cetera). But one cannot simply write about this and be content. It has its pitfalls. One must, naturally, turn his or her gaze to one's private, shared humanity in the daily and the quotidian; just as much as one should turn toward the natural (pomegranate or the sea) and juxtapose it to the categorical or what we sometimes call the specific.

Victims are victims first. We know they are human and humans are neither angels nor saints. There's a fascinating title of a book on the

Rwandan genocide: *When Victims Become Killers*. Obviously this is not just specific to Rwanda. It is a human phenomenon. And yes, victimizers intentionally or otherwise brutalize their victims in order to strip their victims of their humanity and turn them into similar monsters. So to what extent does one fall into the trap of blaming victims? And to what extent does one fall into the trap of apologizing for victims who have become victimizers?

DB: Those are the kinds of questions for which we need art, aren't they? And they are central to your recent poems. How else can we say—how else dramatize—these things in the complexity and uncertainty that they demand?

FJ: One way is to address the politics of naming: what to name, and what to rename. Another way of looking at the name question is to abandon false and presumed identities that are imposed on one as absolutes: nation, religion, and ethnicity. Darwish writes in an elegy to Edward Said, in a dialogue between the two, where the latter says: "Identity is self-defense / and not the inheritance of a past / but what its owner creates."

DB: "Volition is an afterthought." Would you care to pry open that wonderful statement for us here?

FJ: I think this is a parallel syllogism to "the chicken or egg" phenomenon, or the "object" and "the object as an act of consciousness." I am interested in consciousness and its dialectic, because it is another of the significant representations of our contemporary moment, laden with its scientific aura.

DB: Another of your poetic vocations, Fady, is to translate Arabic poetry into English. Your book of Darwish's poems has been really well received. It gathers three individual volumes of his, if I'm not mistaken. Can you place these *Kenyon Review* translations in his timeline? Are they recent, older? To me the prose poems feel distinctly different from "At a Train Station," and perhaps that's due to some slippage in time as well as the obvious formal differences.

FJ: All of the poems are recent. In fact, "At a Train Station" was written at the time of the sixtieth anniversary of the Palestinian dispossession, Nakba, last year, months before Darwish's death. Its conversational discourse, between the narrative, the descriptive, and the expository, is also a recent development in Darwish's longer poems; his sense of the lyric has changed, as does the diction of all great poets in their late style. Soon, I hope, it will become clear to many who read Darwish which era is a given poem written in: his diction and breath and lyric have clear and distinct shifts in them throughout the years.

The prose poems are also recent, from his last collected book *The Trace of the Butterfly (Athar al-Farasheh)* in 2007. He calls them diaries and not poems. In them he experiments openly and persistently with non-prosody. In fact he wrote a memoir in 2006, *In the Presence of Absence,* which reads like a book-long prose poem, a description that made him happy. Darwish always worked at redefining prosody and rhythm in the contemporary Arabic poem, always negotiating the meaning of "free" in poetry. He resisted the notion that modern poetry or free verse meant "free for all." In the same book, he has another prose piece, "In Madrid," in which he recalls reading with Mark Strand, and asking him about what defines a poem away from prosody: And Mark's reply: "rhythm . . . rhythm."

DB: These prose poems also have a kind of interior voice or perspective to them that feels more contented with their interiority. They are not necessarily so social. "So what if I am alone," he says in "If I Were Another."

FJ: Darwish loved his solitude, tried to protect it as much as he could, and only when he realized in 1999 that his days are numbered (after surviving cardiovascular death for the second time in his life) he began to write with a hunger that humanizes himself more and more. He wanted to gaze at the almond blossoms and not have his humanity consumed and eaten up by the checkpoint and the violence of occupation, as he said in 2005. Darwish had also begun to home in on his Sufi gaze in his later years, a presence and a process that had initially surfaced in 1990 in his masterpiece lyric epic *The Hoopoe.* But that is another story. Still, I would like to argue that his interiority had always been there.

By the way I am also glad to say I have a new translation collection of Darwish's lyric epics due this fall from Farrar Straus & Giroux; its title is *If I Were Another.* How about that for a coincidence? In fact, this expression is found in "In Jerusalem," Darwish's poem the *Kenyon Review* published a few years ago. It is an expression, a concept that typifies Darwish's incessant dialogue with and recognition of the "other" who constitutes the self, the "I" in being.

DB: That is a wonderful coincidence! I'm eager to see your new collection of his lyric epics.

I guess you can tell that these two prose poems really surprised me. I didn't know he wrote prose poems. They bear some of the parable-like quality that I love in Paz's prose poems, I think. Both writers impel an intense, compacted impulse toward philosophy in their prose poems. And a deepened metafictional content.

FJ: I remember Darwish telling me with a certain satisfaction how he was awarded an honorary doctorate of philosophy from the University of Chile in Santiago, also back in 1990, on the eve of the death of his friend Yannis Ritsos. Darwish wedded contemporary philosophy with the philosophic traditions of Arabic and Islamic poets and thinkers from the medieval times, including those of Persia and Andalusia, as well as the literary traditions of Sufi writing.

On a related note, there is a wondrous book by Adonis, *Sufism and Surrealism,* that parallels the two movements' similarities although they are ten centuries apart. I think it is a great window to a better, more complete and less self-referential understanding of Arabic literature in English.

DB: Can you identify for us the Sufi element in Darwish's poems?

FJ: "If I Were Another," that alterity, is an important essence of the Sufi element. Sufi poets and masters arose as an alternative to the dogma of mainstream, institution of language and arts (and politics) in the early days of the Islamic empire. One can say they were language poets in a manner of speaking, but they always infused the deconstruction of meaning with a palpable spirituality. Another way of saying this perhaps is how Darwish often brings the self to the brink of its "other" and in doing so achieves forgetting or vanishing into the other. His diction and meaning are between the concrete and the ethereal, a powerful singularity and independence that protect the self from being appropriated by the "other," while freely giving itself over to the other. In his last epic poem, *The Dice Player,* his own elegy weeks before he died, he writes: "My lexicon is Sufi / my desires, sensory / and I am not who I am until the two meet: / I and the feminine I."

DB: For you, in your thorough sense of Darwish's work, how do his prose poems add to his poetic oeuvre? What does he do in them that is specific to them?

FJ: Darwish expanded his themes in them, as you mentioned, and his personal oscillation between metaphysics and existentialism. The "I" is simply merged into two, and not necessarily a "we" (this is more powerful in the original Arabic since there exists a dual nominative case). He also, obviously, abandoned prosody, yet was able to remain lyrical. This is an obsession and a fear of Darwish's: how to continually widen the lyric and in doing so reinvent or reinvigorate prosody; or as the epigraph to his

2005 collection reads, quoting another medieval Arabic scholar: "The best speech is that whose prosody is like prose, and whose prose is like prosody." This is an accomplishment he achieves in "At a Train Station," which reads in Arabic in the same "prosaic" bend as it does in English, to my ears.

DB: In your opening remark you mentioned the tension in Arabic poetry between prosody and prose. I know that Darwish's work is considered, in Arabic, fairly strict in its formality. Could you provide our readers (and me) with a quick lesson? What is free taf'eelah? Am I right in thinking that this form of metrics considers the prosody of a whole stanza—the wholeness of it—rather than of the line itself?

FJ: First, I would say Darwish is considered fairly innovative in his formalism, and not strict in that prohibitive sense. In this he shares much with the brilliant Iraqi poet, Saadi Yussef, who takes the art of prosody to enviable heights, by Darwish's own testimony.

As for the "free taf'eelah," you are correct. It is kin to saying the whole stanza is made up of an even (or whole or divisible) number of feet. However in Arabic there is a recurring scansion or a mixture thereof. But thinking of it with or without a recurring pattern of feet opens up the meaning of "free verse," doesn't it? Is there a poem that doesn't add up to a whole number of feet?

Darwish's magic was in the deceptive simplicity of his language. He adapted the contemporary spoken and written Arabic to ancient prosody, and ancient prosody to contemporary Arabic.

DB: Do you find the tension in Arabic poetics similar to the tension in contemporary American poetry, between formal and freed prosodies? I hope I am right in sensing, at least in American poetry, that these automatic divisions are dissolving.

FJ: I think they are similar to a large extent, because both poetics live in the same moment of time. But it is true there is less public debate about it in American poetry than in Arabic poetic circles. But you know the notion we have in America about how our "democratized" poem through "demotic" vernacular comes, in part, from the luxury afforded to a powerful, decadent society of riches. Still I wonder about the meaning of the dominant presence of poets like Walcott, Heaney, Muldoon, and many others.

In general, I am not a proponent of equating or comparing languages because often this leads to a soft jingoism in my opinion. I allude to this in "Twice a River." Language and poetries are, more often than not, as is science, linked to power structures and histories. It becomes inevitably problematic.

DB: But this problematic is central to the task of the translator, isn't it? You embody the vocations of both poet and translator. The translator must deal, as you say, with the comparing of languages.

FJ: One idea of translation is to echo or mimic the unifying aspects of speech in the language centers in the human brain. That is a creative, highly imaginative process that must believe in a beyond of sorts, beyond the dogma of the contemporary diction perhaps, if need be. Still, I know that I would translate Darwish's poetry differently a few years down the line. Language is not fixed. And no reading of any great poetry can be fixed either.

DB: Of course you pursue a vocation beyond poet and translator. You are also a medical doctor. Which came first for you, poetry or medicine? How do you manage to stay so deeply involved with each?

FJ: I think poetry came first. Still, "volition is an afterthought." Poetry comes so early to a child. I suppose an idea of compassion or suffering arrives equally early. Yet its manifestation through lyric is earlier than that of the practicality of medicine. And how do I manage? I think most poets are at least hypomanic.

DB: Medicine seems to me a form of hope. It is a social expression of sympathy and engagement with others. In its best forms, that seems to me very much like political engagement. Would it be fair to say that medicine and politics are closely related in your life, or is that too simple-minded an assessment?

FJ: They have to be closely related. After all, the patient suffers from the classification of suffering, and doctors hold power over patients, and wed science to power appropriately or inappropriately. Of course without the power systems there would be no "modern medicine" as Foucault and others elucidated.

But the ethics of modern medicine are dubious at best, and are concealed (or diluted) under the penumbra of an amazing infrastructure of law and capitalism. I thought you were going to say "medicine and poetry" are closely related, which of course they are, in those exact terms I just mentioned. We talk about how certain poems are political but we rarely mention the political institution that is the poetry establishment.

DB: I think the discussion about the political institutions that support the poetry establishment is intense and is growing. The relation of poetry to the academy, to the market, to advertising—this is of profound import to many poets and critics now. Our freedom to write derives from systems that we are likely to despise, like the military machine-state or Wall Street.

FJ: And it is exactly the same conundrum with medicine. Again, Michel Foucault's *Birth of the Clinic* is a fantastic rendition as well as an allegory of this question.

DB: I guess that people come to you as a physician when something is wrong, when they are experiencing pain or physical ailment. Poetry is also compelled by pain or at least by irritation. We tend not to write when all is well. Is this a useful point of comparison? Physical and metaphysical irritants?

FJ: Of course, the metaphysical here is often a consequence of the physical. But what do we mean by "all" is well: the within or the without? Can the two be separated?

DB: No, they can't be separated. That's also central to your poems. Do your patients, or your medical colleagues, know about your poetry? I guess I'm thinking of William Carlos Williams and his preference for keeping these two kinds of practice separate.

FJ: I keep them separate. Very few patients know about it. Just as very few doctors know, or care, about it.

DB: What does medicine give you for your poetry? And what does poetry give you for medical practice?

FJ: The questions of compassion and suffering, beyond their clichéd, hackneyed consumption, seem endless. I rarely, in my practice in the U.S., seek medical narratives as source for my poems. But the overarching reality of suffering and living is a different matter. I am not sure what my poetry gives to my medicine or takes away from it. We live in an intensely administered world and we are automatons half the time, it seems. Obviously I am somewhat uncomfortable talking about it.

Similarly I am just as uncomfortable these days talking about my experiences with Doctors Without Borders. I am not going back to the "field" anytime soon, mainly because I have a family with two children. Maybe years down the line. All I can say about that experience is that the horror of this hierarchy of suffering in which we live our daily lives rarely leaves me. It is maddening at times. Especially when I ask myself, as a doctor, as one with power, how I partake in it, and how I have partaken in it.

I am the one who "returns" from these sojourns into "suffering," and I get congratulated on it, as if it weren't just a simple act of private common decency, but a heroism that the society to which I return wants to claim as its own (as one once told me: "thanks for doing this in our name"). And to top it all, I make art out of it.

DB: This seems to be the paradox we have arrived at a number of times in this interview: to be inside a system of power and to critique it at the same time. To sympathize with suffering but also to be part of the wielding of power. This conundrum arose when we talked about poetry, and about translation, and about medicine.

If poetry and medicine are both forms of hopeful practice, what are your hopes, Fady?

FJ: I hope to be able to return to medical service in some capacity around the world. I also hope to relocate or reposition my aesthetic past the centrality of suffering at some point. It is natural for the "I" of the "we" to interiorize. It is not sustainable otherwise.

Ted
Kooser

JEFF GLENNON

TED KOOSER is an American original, whose work in poetry is akin to the paintings of Grant Wood and the music of Aaron Copland. Kooser's poetry is regional and realistic, as lean as Shaker furniture, and like Shaker furniture it is a poetry that values aesthetic beauty, formal economy, and practical use.

Ted Kooser was born in 1939, in Ames, Iowa, and received his college education at Iowa State University and the University of Nebraska. Until his retirement in 1999, he worked as an insurance man—a medical underwriter and eventually a public relations executive—in Lincoln, Nebraska. He now lives on an acreage near Garland, Nebraska, and teaches occasionally at the University of Nebraska. Though his early poetry appeared almost exclusively in small literary journals and was published by independent small-press book companies, he has more recently been recognized as one of America's most important poets. From 2004–2006, he served as Poet Laureate of the United States, and his 2004 collection, *Delights & Shadows,* was awarded the Pulitzer Prize.

Among Kooser's many poetry collections are *Official Entry Blank,* University of Nebraska Press, 1969; *Sure Signs: New and Selected Poems,* University of Pittsburgh Press, 1980; *Weather Central,* University of Pittsburgh Press, 1994; and *Delights & Shadows,* Copper Canyon Press, 2004. His three books of nonfiction are *Local Wonders: Seasons in the Bohemian Alps* (2002), *The Poetry Home Repair Manual* (2005), both from University of Nebraska Press, and a collaborative work, *Writing Brave and Free: Encouraging Words for People Who Want to Start Writing,* cowritten with Stephen Cox. In addition to the Pulitzer Prize, he has been awarded the Society of Midland Authors Award, two fellowships from the National Endowment for the Arts, the Nebraska Book Award, and many others.

Kooser's work as poet laureate included his inauguration of the project, American Life in Poetry, which he still maintains. For this free weekly column, Kooser selects a short lyric poem by a contemporary American poet and writes an introductory comment. The mission of the project, Kooser says, is to promote poetry and to create a vigorous presence for poetry in our culture. Hundreds of newspapers participate in American Life in Poetry by printing this column every week. The column has about four million readers.

Success

I can feel the thick yellow fat of applause
building up in my arteries, friends,
yet I go on, a fool for adoration. Do I care
that when it sloughs off it is likely to go
straight to the brain? I am already showing
the first signs of poetic aphasia,
the words coming hard, the synapses
of metaphor no longer connecting.
But look at me, down on my knees
next to the podium, lapping the last drops,
then rolling in the stain like a dog,
getting the smell in my good tweed sport coat,
the grease on my suede elbow patches,
and for what? Well, for the women I walk past
the next morning, the ones in the terminal,
wheeling their luggage, looking so beautifully
earnest. All for the hope that they will
suddenly dilate their nostrils, squeeze
the hard carry-on handles, and rise to
the ripening odor of praise with which I have
basted myself, stinking to heaven.

Splitting an Order

I like to watch an old man cutting a sandwich in half,
maybe an ordinary cold roast beef on whole wheat bread,
no pickles or onion, keeping his shaky hands steady
by placing his forearms firm on the edge of the table
and using both hands, the left to hold the sandwich in place,
and the right to cut it surely, corner to corner,
observing his progress through glasses that moments before
he wiped with his napkin, and then to see him lift half
onto the extra plate that he asked the server to bring,
and then to wait, offering the plate to his wife
while she slowly unrolls her napkin and places her spoon,
her knife and her fork in their proper places,
then smooths the starched white napkin over her knees
and meets his eyes and holds out both old hands to him.

Bad News

Because it arrives while you sleep,
it's the one call you never pick up
on the first ring. In that pause between
the fourth and what would be the fifth,
in the flare of a lamp you've snapped on,
there it is, having waited all night
until it was time to awaken you,
shaping its sentence over and over,
simple old words you lean into
as into a breath from a cave.
And once the news is out, thrown over
your shoulders like a threadbare robe,
you move on cold feet room to room,
feeling as weightless as a soul,
turning on every light in the house,
needing the light all around you
because it's a new day now, though still
in darkness hours before dawn,
a day you'll learn to call *that* day,
the first morning after it happened.

Spanish Lessons

My wife moves room to room,
touching our humble belongings
with a wand of new words—
the iron, the coffee pot, the radio—
making them notice themselves
for the first time in years.
In the kitchen, I hear her
cracking a few round syllables
into a pan of *agua,* followed soon
by a brisk, gutteral bubbling,
and later she's climbing the stairs
with an armload of colorful noises,
dropping a few shaggy petals
on every other step. She's going
to fill the bathtub now and scatter
fresh flowers of language
over the surface, then lie there
steeping among them, calling out
the new names for shampoo,
for bath mat, toilet and toothbrush,
lying there with her ears just out of
the water, loving the echos.

Two Men on an Errand

The younger, a balloon of a man
in his sixties with some of the life
let out of him, sags on the cheap couch
in the car repair shop's waiting room.
Scuffed shoes, white socks, blue trousers,
a nondescript gray winter jacket.
His face is pale, and his balding head
nods with some kind of palsy. His fists
stand like stones on the tops of his thighs—
white boulders, alabaster—and the flesh
sinks under the weight of everything
he's squeezed within them. The other man
is maybe eighty-five, thin and bent
over his center. One foot swollen
into a foam rubber sandal, the other
tight in a hard black shoe. Blue jeans,
black jacket with a semi tractor
appliquéd on the back, white hair
fine as a cirrhus cloud. He leans
forward onto a cane, with both hands
at rest on its handle as if it were
a steering wheel. The two sit hip to hip,
a bony hip against a fleshy one,
talking of car repairs, about the engine
not hitting on all the cylinders.
It seems the big man drove them here,
bringing the old man's car, and now
they are waiting, now they have to wait
or want to wait until the next thing
happens, and they can go at it
together, the younger man nodding,
the older steering with his cane.

Something Just Happens

A Conversation with Ted Kooser

David Baker: Ted, thanks so much for the chance to talk about your five new poems and about your work as a poet and Poet Laureate of the United States. Tim and I will step in and out with questions for you. I'd like to start with "Success," since it suggests issues relating to the public service of the laureate. Is it true that these five poems are the first you wrote and published since the laureateship?

Ted Kooser: Yes, that's right. While I was poet laureate I had very little time for writing, and these five are among a few that I felt worth publishing.

DB: Let's look at the poem here. This is "Success."

> I can feel the thick yellow fat of applause
> building up in my arteries, friends,
> yet I go on, a fool for adoration. Do I care
> that when it sloughs off it is likely to go
> straight to the brain? I am already showing
> the first signs of poetic aphasia,
> the words coming hard, the synapses
> of metaphor no longer connecting.
> But look at me, down on my knees
> next to the podium, lapping the last drops,
> then rolling in the stain like a dog,
> getting the smell in my good tweed sport coat,
> the grease on my suede elbow patches,
> and for what? Well, for the women I walk past
> the next morning, the ones in the terminal,
> wheeling their luggage, looking so beautifully
> earnest. All for the hope that they will
> suddenly dilate their nostrils, squeeze
> the hard carry-on handles, and rise to
> the ripening odor of praise with which I have
> basted myself, stinking to heaven.

This is one of my favorite new poems of yours. I like it in part because of features that I admire in all your best poems—intensity of observation matched with a casual idiom, self-effacement alongside your obvious delight in making, and maybe most, your genius for image and metaphor, metaphor sustained like a metaphysical poet achieving that high trope of conceit. Here, the conceit is of self-basting, celebrity as high cholesterol.

TK: I wrote it in fun, to answer all my friends, who kept asking what it was like to be thrust into celebrity. They knew I am an introvert, and that it would be difficult for me to be a public figure.

DB: For all the obvious good of the laureateship—both for us and for yourself—we can't ignore the complaint in "Success." I think about your larger body of poetry, where the typical Kooser hero or persona is alone, that single soul out in the vast universe of nature and of others. There's a lone student carrying his heavy backpack through the hard wind, there's a man in awe of a stormy landscape, on and on. The pressure on the protagonist of this poem is, of course, public service. He is ironic and reluctant. But he is also delighted by the "ripening odor of praise," even though he knows it will be, so to speak, the death of him.

How did you manage such public life, so many appearances? You have spent a lifetime in a kind of quiet anonymity in Nebraska. Was this a shock to your system? Or did the honor override the shock?

TK: I guess you might say that the honor overrode the shock. I was at first terrified, but I decided that if the Librarian of Congress was willing to take a chance on a poet from the Great Plains, I'd better do the best job I could. So I threw myself into it and pressed forward. In the twenty months while I was in the post I made around two hundred appearances and did one hundred interviews. I talked to little groups and big ones, local book clubs and Rotary and Kiwanis groups, and, of course, to lots of schools, both secondary and college. That activity continues, and I've made another fifty appearances, I'd guess.

Tim Hofmeister: The laureateship gave you a unique opportunity to look at poetry across the country. I know we want to talk more about this in a minute. But first I want to ask a little more about your work as laureate. In fact, what is the nature of the laureateship? Are there official responsibilities and obligations?

TK: The actual obligations are few. The laureate is asked to give a public reading at the opening of each term, in October, and a lecture at the close of the season, in May. In between the laureate has the privilege of giving away two Witter Bynner Fellowships of $10,000 to promising poets. It's optional, but you can also bring poets to read at the Library of Congress, where they're recorded for posterity. Again, I took on a whole lot in addition to these basics. One of the most pleasurable things I did was to invite the singer-songwriter John Prine to the Library to talk about writing songs. I interviewed him on stage in the Coolidge Auditorium and he was the first folksinger who had been there since Woody Guthrie in the 1930s. You can see that interview on the Library's Web site, www.loc.gov.

By the way, the laureateship is in no way connected with the presidency, the executive branch, or even with Congress. Congress appropriates no money for it. It is a privately endowed program at the Library of Congress. I suppose that if the laureate were summoned to the White House and asked to write a poem for the president, somebody might want to do that. Not this guy. I did have one similar opportunity. I had an e-mail one day from a group of Cheney supporters saying if I would be willing to write a poem for Dick Cheney's birthday. And I responded that I would not be available on that occasion. And then after I hit the send button, I realized that there was no date in the invitation at all.

TH: Did you realize you could've had some fun forwarding that e-mail?

TK: I guess it didn't occur to me to do that. I wanted it out of the house as quickly as possible. But the thing is, actually, even if it had happened to be a politician I respected a great deal, I couldn't write a poem like that. Occasional poems simply do not work, and I don't like writing poems on request. I had written a few things for people's weddings and they're okay for that *one* moment, but as works of art, they just don't hold up.

DB: But that is one of the features of the British poet laureate, isn't it? They are obliged to do poems on command and for occasions. That may be—I looked this up—why we no longer remember the work of Laurence Eusden, Colley Cibber, Henry James Pye, and some of the other less famous laureates from Britain.

TK: And they do it for, I think, a small keg or butt of sherry. Yes, well, we'd all agree that the laureates in America have it a lot better.

TH: I'd like to ask what you felt you've learned from being poet laureate about the state of poetry in the United States.

TK: I became convinced fairly early that there is an enormous audience available to us as writers if we want to approach them, to bring them back. These are people who had poetry ruined for them in the public schools by teachers who said, "The following poem has a meaning that I want you to dig out. I have it written down in the back of my Teacher's Guide." And so we fell upon poems as if they were walnuts we had to crack—rather than seeing poems as pleasurable experiences that we can take into our lives and use however we wish. A poem does not have to have *a meaning!*

I don't want to disparage all English teachers because lots of them do wonderful jobs with this kind of thing and really should be sainted. Everywhere I went when I gave a reading—and my work, for those of you who don't know it, is that I really work hard to make it available to kind of a broad, general audience—anyway, everywhere I went, someone would come up after the reading, some guy in the back, with his thumbs in his belt, and say, "My wife dragged me to this thing and you couldn't have gotten me to go to a poetry reading for anything, but I want you to know I had a good time and I'm going to give this poetry stuff a chance." Modernism, the poetry of the twentieth century, beginning at about World War I, did its best to exclude a lot of readers by its difficulty, its elitism.

TH: I know you've said that there are different kinds of poetry in the United States. Don't you think that's a healthy thing in the United States?

TK: Absolutely. I was saying somewhat facetiously that people will, from time to time, ask a question about the "state of American poetry." You can't really talk about it that way because you have these various groups doing things. You have the cowboy poets who are perfectly happy doing what they are doing. They have this big meeting in Nevada every year and they have a wonderful time. You have rap poets who have a big following; you have the hip-hop. You know, all these various groups. All of them are thriving within their groups and they really don't have too much interest in each other.

Shortly after I was named poet laureate, I thought, "I'm going to go to the National Cowboy Poetry thing in Elko, Nevada. That ought to be fun." So I called up the Western Folklife Association that runs it and said I was just appointed Poet Laureate of the United States and I'd like to come to the Elko thing. And the response was, "So what!" They don't care about the Poet Laureate of the United States; they've got their own thing going. All those groups are there, and they are *thriving*. The only group that thinks everyone should be writing like them is us, the literary poets.

DB: Let me ask something related to that. We're talking about school. We're all working in schools. And now you're talking about what happens to poetry in schools. Here are two passages I want to read for your response. This is from Jerry Thompson in the *Yale Review:* "Nabokov wrote that 'Art consists of specific details and not the general ideas Americans are taught from High School to look for in works of art.' He's unquestionably right; the difference between art and commonplace expression is in the last five percent of rigor." And this is Paul Kane: "Since virtually all literary themes can be reduced to commonplaces, there is clearly something other than cognitive content that attracts us."

I'm interested in what that other thing *is*. We get good at asking our students to find the theme of this or that poem. We take a beautiful poem and reduce it to its theme. You know: Nature is awful, nature is beautiful, we are all silly people doomed by fate or culture. . . . So what is it that we're missing in the treatment of poetry in school? What is that "thing" that makes the poem more than its testable content?

TK: I think we respond to poems the same way we respond to works in a gallery. We walk through a gallery; we may not be crazy about abstract expressionism, but we turn the corner in a gallery and there is an abstract expressionist painting, and there's something that just happens to us, and this is an individual, a private response. There are poems that will immediately move us, emotionally move us. And we don't need to know exactly why that happens. I mean we can, upon analysis, figure it out: what is it about that painting that makes it so thrilling, but we have to use language to do that, and our response to a painting is not in language but in the viscera, in the heart.

Allan Grossman has a beautiful poem called "Two Waters." It's one of my favorites. On this farm he's talking about, there are two kinds of water: the water that drained into the cistern from melting snow and falling rain and then the well water, which is of a different character. I think the reason that I love that poem so much is because that's the way it was at my grandparents' home. They had a cistern and a well. It's beautifully written but it also seems to be written for me. I bring my own experience to the poem. I don't know whether that's a decent answer.

DB: It's a fine answer. Your illustration about understanding poetry uses the example of an art gallery. Does your own work as a painter affect your poetry? Are your paintings miniatures, too, like the poems?

TK: I do often paint very small paintings, five inches by seven, say, even smaller. I think a big part of making art of any kind is an attempt to secure order, and there can be a lot of pleasure in making something small and orderly.

TH: I'd like to get back to the issue of audience again, as well. I guess my question would be, "How do we get more people to come out to poetry readings?"

TK: Well, people will read and enjoy poetry and go to poetry readings as long as those experiences are pleasurable. We have to remember that pleasure is an important thing to human beings. We all want to have a pleasurable experience, but to go to a reading where you're sitting in the audience for sixty minutes and someone is reading and not saying anything that you understand in any way is an altogether unpleasant experience. That has happened to a lot of people because of the difficulty and obscurity that evolved in the twentieth century.

In building readership for poetry we have to think of having fun with little children. I really do believe children will be lifelong readers of poetry if we will spend time showing them that it is fun when they are small. A lot of teachers are very good at that, and poets like Shel Silverstein and Dr. Suess can provide material. Their work shows that poetry can be fun.

But all too often what happens is that Ms. Smith in the eighth grade says that the meaning of this poem is not what you said it is; in fact you get a D today because you didn't get the meaning right. So everybody gets out of school and they see a poem in the *New Yorker* and they go, "Ahh, I don't have to do that anymore, I got a D in that."

DB: I want to ask you more about this, the issue of availability. I am thinking about your own style and clarity, the simplicity of style in your poetry. I wonder whether you might agree with this little sentence of Edmund Burke. Burke says that "a clear idea is another name for a little idea."

TK: No, I would not agree. It's great fun not to agree with Edmund Burke.

DB: I thought that is what you might say. Let me trace the tendency toward simplicity back a little farther. Your own style is a plain style or colloquial style, where the lyric poem is stripped down, image driven, and narrative based. So I'm thinking of the American appeal to simplicity that runs all the way back to William Bradford, the first governor of Plymouth. In referring to the need for simplicity in his own language, he says "as by the scriptures we are plainly told." He extols the virtue of simplicity or plainness. This is embedded in our national character, even our politics and religion, and of course in one strain of our poetry.

TK: That Shaker song, "T'is a Gift to Be Simple," might make a good thing to tack up over a writing desk. One of the most influential books for me as a writer is the Strunk and White *Elements of Style*. That book puts a lot of emphasis on the virtues of clarity and simplicity.

DB: Let me ask you to respond to one last quotation. This is Helen Vendler. And the question again is about style, your own. Vendler says that "a writer's true vision lies in the implications of his or her style."

Now, as you think about what your style is or what you hope it is, do you see a connection between style and something larger, like vision?

TK: That's very interesting. I'm not sure what Miss Vendler means, but I do think that style is an extension of personality. I am comfortable, as a person, with the style of my poems, if that makes any sense at all. I am saying poems out of my heart, and this feels harmonious with the person whom I am. I tend to be someone who writes with a great deal of sentiment. I'm willing to take that risk at a time when people are suspicious of sentimental poetry. But I think that is what I need to do as a poet.

DB: Do your think your vision, then, is a social one? Or at least, do you think your style is crafted to be more available and public, rather than exclusive or academic?

TK: Yes, absolutely. Let me turn back to this problem we have with excluding audience. I'd like to be on record as saying that anybody can write a poem that nobody can understand. That's really easy. On the other hand, it might be really hard to write a poem that everyone in a room found meaning in. I would fail at that, even though I would like to reach out to everyone in this room.

TH: I have a question that relates to these issues—of the poet's ability to reach a broad audience, to speak or write in ways that are inclusive versus exclusive. "Availability" doesn't necessarily equate to "ease." Some of your poems that seem accessible are also challenging. I'm thinking of poems like "Praying Hands." You write a lot about hands, but here the hands are a made object. They are akin to particular objects in other poems— broken-down rural churches, odd roadside shrines—with some religious connotation. I wondered why these objects keep coming back into the poetry. My first guess is that they have something to do with what David calls the midwestern social text; these objects are a part of the community and they need to be represented.

TK: I'm not a traditional believer in any manner of speaking, but I do go to church, I go to different churches. I like sitting with a group of people for about an hour who I imagine are thinking in the right direction. The denomination means nothing to me; it's the idea of being in a community. People who are actually spending some time thinking about their spiritual life.

When I was younger I was extremely intolerant of people who were devout believers. I have come to believe that nearly everyone is trying to live a good life, and this may be tremendously Pollyanna-ish of me to think this. There are a few evil people in the world and they cause a lot of trouble, but nearly everyone is trying to live a good life despite ignorance and poverty and the worst kind of circumstances.

Several years ago, I went to a wedding where the brother of the bride was a jailor in Texas, at the county facility that processes all the prisoners going to their executions at Huntsville. Now as you know—I hope you know—Texas executes maybe a hundred and fifty people a year, and Huntsville is where that happens. So these prisoners are coming to this country facility to be processed before they are sent on to death row. I said, "How many of these people are genuinely evil?" He said, "Ted, maybe one or two out of one hundred." He said the rest of them have just made stupid choices.

We might make fun of somebody with a *Praying Hands* plaque on his wall. But I'm for kindness and tolerance toward all of those things; they're part of what we have and who we are. The world is too short of kindness.

TH: You write quite a few poems about nature and seem to imply there is an order of things in nature. By contrast, in "The Red Wing Church," there's a sort of comedy going on. The church is all busted up, it's disintegrating and you find the pews on everybody's porches around town, and the cross is God knows where. On the other hand, in a passage from *Local Wonders* you carefully depict the Mennonite women, whose community is intact, and you invest them with a lot of respect. You begin by saying, "A person needn't be fearful of sixty-five-year-old Mennonite women in white lace caps." This implies, correctly, I think, that there is a lot of fear on the part of many people of other people who are like the Mennonite women.

TK: I know nothing about the Mennonite religion really. All I have to draw on is that when I go into the store and those women are behind the counter, I like the way they count out the change. They're so careful not to cheat me of a penny. We really have a wonderful country full of lots of fascinating, beautiful people. I think we have a lot of stupidity in our leaders, but most of the people, I think, are pretty good people, doing as best they can.

TH: A certain kind of poetic approach can challenge a reader with a vision of inclusion, and at a time when the country is divided in so many ways—Nascar Nation, *New Yorker* Nation, and so on. It's as if we've reached a point where people want to say, thanks to social stratification or the legal system or whatever, we are finally immune from one another. A sad view, really, which I find your poems often subvert.

DB: These issues—of clarity, inclusion, public utility—must be related to your work with American Life in Poetry. Would you say something about that? How did your project get started? What have been your goals? And what do you see for the future of the project?

TK: My wife is in the newspaper business, and for years she and I had been talking about how one might get poetry back into the papers. There was a time when lots of newspapers printed poetry. It was her idea to let papers use the column free. She didn't think that, on the lean budgets upon which newspapers now operate, many could pay even five dollars a week. We wanted it to be free. After I was made poet laureate I approached the Poetry Foundation. Without them it couldn't have happened. They were behind the creation of the Web site and they continue to maintain it. And they have given me enough money to pay for a halftime assistant editor and a graduate assistant. I get no money from them, but that's fine. I am a volunteer. The column has been very successful, and at the time of this interview we have about four million readers. We have been published in around three hundred papers. I plan to keep the column going as long as I can, and, of course, as long as the Poetry Foundation continues to support it. What the column accomplishes is to show American newspaper readers that poetry is not something they need to fear, that there are poems that can be understood and appreciated.

DB: Let's backtrack now—to before the laureateship and the Pulitzer. Once upon a time, you were an insurance man back home in Lincoln. How did your work in business affect the poetry?

TK: I believe that writers write for perceived communities, and that if you are a lifelong professor of English, it's quite likely that you will write poems that your colleagues would like, that is, poems that will engage that community. I worked every day with people who didn't read poetry, who hadn't read it since they were in high school, and I wanted to write for them. I am not looking for an audience of literary professionals, though it's nice when some of them like what I'm doing.

DB: And you retired, I think, around 2000?

TK: In mid-1998 I was diagnosed with a squamous cell tongue carcinoma that had spread into my neck. I never returned to work after that. I was able to retire at age sixty about six months later, after an extensive sick leave. I'm delighted to say that I am cured now, I'm well, but it was a bad thing to go through. And it was the end of my insurance career, but I have never missed it for a minute.

As I began to come out of that illness, the University of Nebraska asked me to do some more teaching. I had, from time to time, taught as an adjunct. So they brought me in as a visiting professor. Later I was made Presidential Professor and given a renewable contract. Anyway. the insurance career was over in 1999. I had been just doing what I do, writing poems and painting pictures and doing a little bit of teaching. Then this poet laureate thing came out of the blue and I decided it was an opportunity to make some statements about poetry and talk to people in the world about American poetry. I took this on and I worked pretty much seven days a week for two years. It was very important for me to show that someone from Nebraska could do that kind of work.

TH: That's a pretty amazing commitment of time and energy. Are you still working so hard?

TK: Now that I am out of office, I feel a little bit more able to say "no" to things even though I am always honored when I am asked to come to some civic group or something or other like that. I still do a lot of that. But I'm trying to say "no" a little more because I need to get back to doing some writing and quiet down a little. I keep my calendar on a word-processing document; and at the height of my activity, I had five pages of things to do, single spaced. It's down to about two and a half now. Over the next year or so, I hope to get back to where I can spend more time at home, where I write best, and I can do some painting. I'm still teaching. I teach once a year in the fall semester, just one class, and I'll keep doing that. And then my newspaper column is something that doesn't take up a great deal of time, but I do have to put regular time on that during the week.

DB: So now, what is a normal day like for you, what is your habit and what do you expect out of yourself?

TK: Well, all those years when I was at the insurance company I learned that if I was going to do any writing at all, I had to do it early in the morning. And I got up at 4:30 a.m. every day, and I would write until maybe 7:00. Then I would get in and out of the shower and get my suit and tie on and go off to the insurance company. And I have continued that all these years. You know, once you get use to getting up at 4:30 in the morning, that's when you get up. My dogs are used to getting up at that time and if I don't get up, they're usually bothering me to get up. So I get up every morning and I sit in the same chair every morning, with my coffee pot at hand and write in a notebook.

And I am a dismal failure as a writer twenty-eight days out of thirty. It's just junk when I'm done, after my two or three hours at it. But I've learned that unless I'm sitting there with my notebook, on the day when the good one comes, I'm never going to get it at all. So I have to show up for work, which is one of the important things about doing this kind of work, or doing really any work.

Here is a little anecdote. This happened just before Thanksgiving one year. I had broken an overhead door in one of the outbuildings on my farm and I went to the lumberyard to find a part for it. Here was this older guy who knows where things are, and he's sorting through all these boxes, and we started to talk about Thanksgiving coming. He said it was going to be a warm Thanksgiving and so he was going to pitch horseshoes after Thanksgiving dinner. I said something about horseshoe pitching and about the fact that I had an uncle with cerebral palsy who could barely walk but who could pitch horseshoes. He said, "Yeah, my uncle Ed was Tri-State Horseshoe Pitching Champion three years running, and I asked my uncle, 'Uncle Ed, how did you get so good?' And he said, 'Son, you gotta pitch a hundred shoes a day.'"

That's what it takes to get good at anything. You've got to be in there pitching horseshoes every day. If at the end of the year I've written ten poems that I think are really effective, then it's a really good year for me—six to ten.

DB: How do you *know* your good poems? How do they assert themselves or stand out from the other ones? In horseshoes, it's clear. The thrower hears the ping and sees the shoe around the peg.

TK: Sometimes I don't know. I have a sense of the quality of the work when it's finished. Maybe it's a ping. I want every part to snap into place at some point and become a whole. That poem "Success" is a good example. Or a poem David has written about, "Etudes," which is as strong a poem as I've ever written. From the minute I wrote it I was delighted with it, with finishing it. I remember thinking, "Did I just write this thing?" I was astounded at the way it all came together. So you have the feeling every once in a while when it all comes together and it feels like more than itself somehow.

DB: On those two poems, can you say what it is that came together, or why a particular poem may seem like your best one?

TK: I think what happens is in that extended metaphor. The power is in having its parts, its vehicle and tenor, greatly separated and then moved into a relationship. In "Etude," we have a bird, a blue heron, and we have a guy sitting in a blue suit at a desk. It's a big stretch to make. And if you try a stretch like that with a metaphor, and you can't hold it up, it will just sag and fall away. It happens that in that poem I was somehow able to make it work. I do believe that a lot of this material or connection comes forth by dictation; something deep in me, something that I'm not really in control of. If I knew how to write a poem like that, I would do it every day. But I can't. What happens in my favorite ones is that, toward the end of the poem, the metaphor makes a circle, it goes way out here, way at this guy at the desk, and it comes back at the point where I say, "his pencil poised in the air like the beak of a bird." Back we'll go to the heron and then it's all over. The figure is complete.

I have no idea how I wrote that, but I had to be sitting there for a long time to do it just so.

DB: We have talked a lot about plainness. But in some way, your best poems move beyond conventional definitions of the plain. I am thinking of what you have described just now, that sustained or pushed metaphor. Isn't that a very fanciful figurative metaphysical conceit, where you take an image and push it into a metaphor and take the metaphor and push it into a pattern, and push the pattern as far as it will possibly go until it nearly breaks? That's the way you were talking about the heron poem and that's what I see in "Success" and, really, the other four poems here. "Success" is not an imagist poem so much as a poem of conceit. "Two Men on an Errand" works that way, too. It develops an image—the men waiting at an auto repair shop—but pushes the whole image into metaphor and the metaphor into sustained conceit. There's a "foam rubber sandal," which seems like a car tire, and the older man "steering with his cane," and much more. This extends far beyond the simplicity of an isolate image. It seems to me, in some way, not plain at all. Is that a fair thing to say, or is that an insult?

TK: No, it isn't plain in the common sense, and I thank you for describing it so clearly. I think one thing about working with metaphor this way is that you want both sides to work perfectly well together. It's a matter of paring away the things that won't work in the comparison and being sure that the only things in the comparison are ones that play on both sides. Often, most of my work goes into fine tuning the central metaphor.

DB: You pare away? So perhaps you achieve a kind of plainness or economy even in the way you construct patterns of metaphor. No waste, even in elaboration.

TH: It almost seems as though the breaking point between a plain style and another kind of style is metaphor. But maybe you're saying it's more the way you manage the metaphor?

TK: I don't know, Tim. I guess the plain style is there in that I'm going for simplicity and plainness and clarity.

DB: The rhetoric is plain, the idiom. That's the virtue of the plain style in your poems. But the application of the metaphor, the pushing of metaphor into extended conceit, that's the thing I like, that sort of irony, that pull of those two polarities. What we think of as usually different kinds of rhetoric. It shoves the image beyond its economical spare use.

TH: I'm thinking of a passage in *Local Wonders* where you're talking to your postman. Your postman has seen one of your poems and also some mention of your poetry and he reluctantly says, "They say you have a gift for metaphor." What exactly does that mean? What I like about that passage is you work through with him what metaphor is and what metaphor does. And that contributes to a step in his understanding of what you're about.

TK: I can't remember exactly how that passage goes, but the mailman had stopped me by the side of the road and said he read on the back of a book that I was a "master of metaphor" and he said, "What does that mean?" I said, "Well, you know, a metaphor is a kind of comparison of things." He said, "You mean when I say such and such was like, it was like . . . well, you know what I mean." I said, "Yeah, that's right."

TH: Do we have a natural gift for metaphor and to what extent, do you think?

TK: No, all of us don't have a natural gift for metaphor. I happen to be blessed with an imagination that leans in that direction. I've worked with a lot of students who have learned to write poems that exclude metaphors because they are just no good at it. You cannot deliberately construct a metaphor. It arises in the process of writing. It always comes as a marvelous surprise when it arrives. Just like that "Etude" poem, you think, "Where did that come from?" A student will show me a poem and say, "Don't you think I ought to put a metaphor right about there?" As if you could go to Circuit City and buy one and plug it in. I am immensely grateful that I was given an imagination that has the associative side to it.

TH: You have a wonderful way of sharing it in the poems. This partly has to do with what we are talking about, with that style. I also think about a device you use, which I think we have touched on. Where you say to a reader "you've seen how" and then you lead them into a scene. But you have a tension there, too, a tension where you expect a person to say, "Yes, I have seen that."

TK: You have to be careful with that kind of "lead-in" phrase. In the poem we're talking about—it's the one about the woman in the wheelchair, in which I say, "You've seen how pianists bend forward to strike the keys, then lift their hands." I can assume when I write like that every one here has seen a pianist do that. I wouldn't say, "You've seen how a man can repair a carburetor on a chainsaw." I couldn't expect you to know that.

There is another poem, the kind of poem that we've been talking about, a poem with an extended metaphor, that I sometimes read in public. It's called "A Washing of Hands." This is what happens to me when I'm working. I try to pay attention. This is the important thing in being a writer, trying to pay attention to what's going on. I was watching my wife at the sink washing her hands under the water and then flicking her fingers to get the water off.

DB: Great. Let's take a look at "A Washing of Hands."

> She turned on the tap and a silver braid
> unraveled over her fingers.
> She cupped them, weighing that tassel,
> first in one hand and then the other,
> then pinched through the threads
> as if searching for something, perhaps
> an entangled cocklebur of water,
> or the seed of a lake. A time or two
> she took the tassel in both hands,
> squeezed it into a knot, wrung out
> the cold and the light, and then, at the end,
> pulled down hard on it twice,
> as if the water were a rope and she was
> ringing a bell to call me, two bright rings,
> though I was there.

TK: I love the idea of playing your way into that sort of associative stuff: just a braid of water. Those are the kinds of poems I really love to write because I am always so thrilled when they work. And let down when they fail.

DB: This poem again is a single conceit, or rather, a poem whose metaphor keeps transforming into another version of itself. There's the cocklebur, and then the seed of the lake, and then the tassel, the knot, the rope. There images aren't exactly cognitively connected; it's more about the magic, the leap of an associative imagination.

TK: Yes, it's me following my imagination as it plays, and writing down some of that play, but not all of it. In a poem like that I will usually have deleted some of the play if it doesn't seem to enhance the effect. I like your use of the word magic, because when those metaphors come to me, unbidden, it feels magical.

DB: What do you see as the most hopeful movements in contemporary poetry? You are right, earlier, when you point out so many fields and schools and types. A poetry for every audience. There is a loud din in the small world of poetry. What do you foresee?

TK: I am not much of a scholar, and no cultural historian, but I hope time will somehow preserve the poems that have real meaning for broad groups of people, not just for literary professionals. Sir Thomas Beecham once said that he thought composers should write music that chauffeurs and delivery boys could whistle. Elsewhere he said that unless composers write music that organ grinders can play it will never be immortal.

DB: What are you working on now? I know—the American Life in Poetry project. But how about your poems? Are you writing? Do you see a new collection in the future?

TK: I am slowly assembling a small stack of poems I'm pleased with, and the ones in the *Kenyon Review* are part of that, but I think it will be five or six years before I have another book ready. I don't want to publish anything that isn't at least as well done as *Delights & Shadows*. Right now, I could get just about anything published because my name is well known. But it would be stupid to use that celebrity as a way of getting inferior work published. Others have done that and it's a mistake.

TH: I wonder if you have any final things you'd like to say—about your work, or the wider state of poetry?

TK: Poetry has meant a great deal to me for almost fifty years, and I have been immensely lucky with my poems, to have them noticed and appreciated. I have a happy writing life and I am thankful.

W. S.
Merwin

MATT SCHWARTZ

W. S. MERWIN has been at the forefront of American poetry since the first appearance of his work in the early 1950s, helping to shape the subjects and forms of the art through the last sixty years. His most recent book of poems, *The Shadow of Sirius,* won the 2010 Pulitzer Prize, joining his 1971 volume, *The Carrier of Ladders,* in that honor. He is one of the most highly celebrated poets in American literary history. In 2010 Merwin was named Poet Laureate of the United States.

W. S. Merwin was born in 1926 in New York City and grew up in New Jersey and Pennsylvania. After graduating from Princeton University, he lived in Europe, where he commenced a career in literary translation. His first book of poems, *The Mask of Janus,* was selected by W. H. Auden for the Yale Series of Younger Poets Prize in 1952, and since then he has published dozens of books, not only of poetry but also of autobiographical and creative nonfiction as well as many books of translations. His translations include work from a rich variety of languages, including

French, Spanish, Italian, Latin, and several Asian languages, and range from epic poems to tiny "figures," from classical drama to surreal lyrics.

Merwin's own poetry has helped to lead American poets through a vast evolution. His early work is remarkable for its formal virtuosity and classical bearing. In the 1960s, following the influence of several Spanish poets, he helped to forge the Deep Imagist movement with poetry notable for its austere, fabular primitivism and its political aptitude. Since then his work has ranged from personal narratives and open forms to work in syllabics and in lyrics informed by environmental and social concerns. Since 1976 Merwin has lived in Hawaii, where he first traveled to study Zen Buddhism and where he currently lives on an old pineapple plantation at the edge of a dormant volcano. Here he works with his wife, Paula, to restore the land and to tend an acreage of rare and endangered palm trees.

The present interview was begun in the studios of Bloomberg News in New York City and is a conversation among Merwin, David Lynn (editor of the *Kenyon Review*), and this book's editor. This event was part of the *Kenyon Review*'s tenth anniversary celebration of the KR Lifetime Achievement Award, presented in 2010 to W. S. Merwin.

Homecoming

Once only when the summer
was nearly over and my own
hair had been white as the day's clouds
for more years than I was counting
I stood by the garden at evening
Paula was still weeding around
flowers that open after dark
and I looked up to the clear sky
and saw the new moon and at that
moment from behind me a band
of dark birds and then another
after it flying in silence
long curving wings hardly moving
the plovers just in from the sea
and the flight clear from Alaska
half their weight gone to get them home
but home now arriving without
a sound as it rose to meet them

From the Gray Legends

Arachne wove the gray before daylight
from beyond the screen of fronds
before the birds before words
before the first stories
before voices
before Minerva's eyes were made
of that same gray
Arachne had her own beauty
seen or unseen
and she was older
she was already who she was
then it was day
and Minerva wove in the daylight
from daylight
and she knew where the threads
were going in their stories
some of them
some of the time
and she claimed that she always knew
Arachne claimed nothing
Arachne did not have to know
she could wait
even when she was forgotten
and she could wait to be forgotten
Minerva kept seeing Arachne's weaving
waiting in the daylight
with the daylight passing through it
the weaving reminded Minerva of something
she could not see there
that she could not remember
Arachne's weaving
even where it was broken
was always perfect
with a perfection that Minerva
could not trace nor imitate

her own wisdom laughed at her
and she was angry
what could she do to Arachne
who could weave the gray before daylight
she started the story
about a contest between them
which she won
weaving daylight
and then what could she do
to Arachne to obliterate her
to forget her
as though she had never existed
all day in Minerva's own mind
in her own weaving in her own dream
she could not imagine a way
to unmake Arachne
all night her own bird answered only
Who
the bird knew
she could not change Arachne
into anything but Arachne
in the gray before day
wherever Minerva's gray eyes turned
she saw Arachne's weaving

Before Midsummer above the River Again

Unseen words
thoughts of words
circle the empty room
where I was young
stars in daytime
that old
not a sound from them
not one question
hey know me
in their unseen galaxy
they are my own
the walls that were
whitewashed in another age
have turned into
maps of shadows
through half my life
and more
my dog three years gone
and more
oh more
barks in a dream
beside my left hand
watchful as ever
waking me
from that dream
where is she
where am I

By the Front Door

Rain through the morning
and in the long pool an old toad singing
happiness old as water

Leave the Door Open

A Conversation with W. S. Merwin

David Lynn: My name is David Lynn, and I am the editor of the *Kenyon Review*. David Baker and I will be chatting with W. S. Merwin, the current Poet Laureate of the United States, and also the recipient of the 2010 Kenyon Review Award for Literary Achievement.

Mr. Merwin, would you like to begin this conversation by reading a poem?

W. S. Merwin: I would be happy to. I think, perhaps since it's a rainy day outside, a good one would be "Rain Light" from *The Shadow of Sirius,* my last published book.

> All day the stars watch from long ago
> my mother said I am going now
> when you are alone you will be all right
> whether or not you know you will know
> look at the old house in the dawn rain
> all the flowers are forms of water
> the sun reminds them through a white cloud
> touches the patchwork spread on the hill
> the washed colors of the afterlife
> that lived there long before you were born
> see how they wake without a question
> even though the whole world is burning

DL: That's a beautiful poem.

David Baker: Nine syllables in every line, William. You've been counting for a long time. Your first books often featured syllabic or metrical poems, and you returned to syllabics again in books like *The River Sound* (1999) and again lately as this poem shows. Nine is an unusual number for syllables, isn't it? Do you tend to prefer an odd numbered line or an even-numbered line?

WM: You know, it varies. I think there's something to be said for any number of syllables, but I've always been watchful of iambic pentameter all of my life. I admire it enormously. I realize that it's an important form, but it has become one of those imports that has taken over, starting with Chaucer. We think of it as natural. The French, oddly enough, had a ten-syllable line when *The Song of Roland* was written. *The Song of Roland* is in a ten-syllable line, but mostly the French go for a twelve-syllable line, the Italians an eleven-syllable line, and somewhere along the line you want to shake the whole thing up. I mean, I did.

DB: *Roland* was one of your own first translations, as I recall. I'd like to ask more about your translations soon. But first a memory. The last time you and I talked about poetry you were hanging over a fence, visiting my new colt, Mercury. That was ten years ago in Granville, Ohio. I have a photo of your hand reaching out—you were wearing my old barn coat. I have a picture of the sleeve and Mercury is reaching out to sniff your hand and his nose is going down into the grass. I don't think I ever sent you that photo. It is really nice to have this chance to talk to you.

WM: I loved Mercury.

DB: With the Kenyon Review Award for Literary Achievement and all the festivities tonight in New York and to continue this weekend into Gambier, David wanted to ask a question about Mr. Ransom.

DL: You have such a long history with the *Kenyon Review.* You've been publishing in its pages for over fifty years. We have at Kenyon some of your correspondence with Mr. Ransom, founder and editor of the *Kenyon Review* for twenty years. I wonder if you have any thoughts about him or memories of him as an editor and as a poet.

WM: As a poet, particularly. I remember reading his criticism of that kind, the New Critics. I think he may have been the best of them all. Richard Blackmur, who was my mentor, was not one of the New Critics. He was completely on his own. But I liked Ransom's essays. I don't think the theories would have lasted very long with me. But what I knew about him as a man, everything I ever heard about him, sounded just wonderful, and the correspondence was wonderful.

I love his poems. I'm very sad that he's as little read as he is.

DL: Do you think that's a matter of being mostly formal, his poems, or has the sensibility of our time changed so much?

WM: Probably both. I think the sensibility of our time may be simply a matter of the generations. I'm suspicious, and that is a part of my generation: I know I'm suspicious of the world, of virtual reality, and of being sucked into it. And I think that the poems of the young poets (and I think there is a great deal of talent around) . . . but the young poets who have grown up writing on an electronic medium, something is happening to their hearing. They don't hear. And poetry begins with the light but it has to begin with the light of *hearing* it. I think that is one of the conditions of poetry. I don't think poetry is the printed word. I think poetry may, eventually, be the printed word, but it is really the spoken word to begin with.

DB: Could you say more about that, the printed word and the heard word?

WM: One of the big differences between poetry and prose is that. To me, the reason I'm so anxious is because, in the very whole of my experience with poetry, going back to when I was a child, the love of poetry came from hearing poems, not from listening to somebody talk about them. But hearing the King James translation of Psalms, hearing the hymns in church, hearing my mother read Tennyson, the books of Robert Louis Stevenson. So the first poems that came to me came to me as words that I heard, to be written down and then be pondered and listened to, to see where they were on their way to.

DL: You speak with passion about this. Let me follow up just for a second, because your decision to agree to be the poet laureate, in some ways, seems strange and anomalous, since you've spent your career as a very private person and man and poet, writing your way in your own places. Now you've accepted this very public role. I wonder if what you are talking about is one of the reasons you've done this.

WM: I think it is. I think also I've always shied away from anything, any position of that kind. But when it was proposed to me at the end of April this year, the piece of luck, if it was luck, if it was a good decision, is that I was given a month to think about it.

I said some things right at the beginning. I said I don't want to live in Washington, I don't want to spend my lifetime in Washington, and I don't want to be taking a lot of trips from Hawaii to other places. I know where I want to live.

And I'm homesick even if I go into town to buy vegetables. I love our way of living and looking out of the windows at trees on every side. I've always wanted to do that, ever since I was a child, and I don't feel like leaving it at all.

But I thought it's a chance to say in a public place, in an official capacity, something that I don't hear anybody else saying clearly. I mean, people are preaching about it on the one hand, and people are ignoring it on the other, but how about just coming out and saying it, and saying it in connection with poetry, and with poetry and the imagination. That's why I took the job: because I think the imagination is *the* talent we have as a species. Not the intelligence. We may not *be* the smartest, yet that's how we certainly define our superiority, and it is always we who do the defining. I'm suspicious of that.

DL: I heard you talking about that recently, and I wondered if you could say a little bit more. You talk about imagination as defining us as humans, but could you talk more about the urge to express ourselves through the imagination or where that comes from, or how it manifests itself in your work?

WM: You know, I don't think it needs to be something that has to be there, like a religious dogma or belief, and I certainly don't want to preach and I don't want to write propaganda. I don't want to think of it that way. But to me it's not that there's a connection, it's that there's no separation. I think that the artificial thing is the idea that there *is* a separation. And there is something very dangerous in that, as that quite late verse in the Book of Genesis says, "You must now multiply and have dominion over all the creatures of the earth."

There was a man who came to talk with me very recently, a Hebrew scholar, and he said, "You know that word 'dominion'? It has another meaning which was never mentioned around the translations. It also means 'understanding.'" One should understand the other creatures of the earth, and that kind of a relationship.

DL: That's wonderful.

WM: Yes, it is wonderful. There are many different kinds of relations with the rest of life that we are not encouraged to have. One of the reasons is because, once you enter into the thing of exploiting them and treating them as dollars and cents or something to put on the plate, you're not likely to look at them in quite the same way. I don't think any of these are neat questions with neat, dogmatic answers, but I think one should leave the question open, keep it open, remain troubled by it, perhaps, and allow it to go on asking itself.

DB: We've galloped through several topics, and I'd like to slow down. I'd like to ask about your attitude or vision of what you want this laureateship to be, and the odd predicament of a public position for this fairly private enterprise, the writing of poems. I want to talk about that, and I want to talk about a little bit more in a minute about young poets. You were talking about some poverty of imagination, their incapability to hear or to express a sort of aural or audible imagination rather than a visual one.

But I think the question I want to ask you right now is just about your own work and your own practice. Whether writing a poem is a daily practice for you, whether it's part of a larger spiritual practice for you, whether you revise a great deal or not, whether anybody helps you with your poems. How do you write a poem?

WM: I don't know where a poem comes from. And I think that's very important. I try, at least, sometime every day, and as early as possible in the morning, to spend some time in the place where I've been able to hear poems, maybe looking at some notes that I've made about poems or something of the kind.

I don't work on a computer. I work on a little spiral notebook. And I obviously didn't think I was going to do anything this morning, because I realize I left it in the room, I didn't bring it with me. So, you asked me if I worked every day.

DB: Yes.

WM: I try to go near it in one way or another and leave it open—leave the door open— and see what I hear.

DB: You've said now two or three times that, as a poem comes to you, you will *hear* the poem. What do you hear?

WM: At some point Yeats one day heard, "That is no country for old men."

DB: He heard it intact.

WM: Yes, just like that. And they were words which he'd used all his life. He may have even heard that phrase all his life. Never thought anything of it, but all of a sudden the light went on. And he thought—well, he spent the next two and a half years writing that poem. And it is one of the great poems, I think, in modern English.

To me, poetry *is* physical, it *is* hearing, and we hear it and the charge, the power, the hypnotic power or grasp of poetry is there, just as it is in music. I mean, there is a musical side to poetry, and I'm not talking about how lovely Swinburne sounds or something like that. I mean that thing— what Yeats heard when he heard that phrase—that is all the way through the poem. It's a great, great poem.

I realized years later that I'd had that poem memorized for twenty years and I'd never stopped to think what it meant. I went back and I picked it apart, looked at it carefully, and it was absolutely wonderful. I didn't even need to know that because I knew it from hearing it.

There's that wonderful phrase Phillip Sydney has in "An Apology for Poetry" where he says, "Poetry begins in delight and ends in wisdom."

The thing is that people are happy enough to talk about how it ends in wisdom, whatever that may mean, but they don't dwell enough, I think, on the delight. The delight was obvious enough for the Puritans so that they closed the theaters and forbade poetry. *We don't want that—*

DB: That's right.

WM: And when people say they don't read poetry because they don't understand it, I think in the first place, they mean they don't hear it anymore, and in the second place, the delight got lost somewhere along the way. And if you liked it, you were discouraged from liking it. It's quite easy to discourage a child, you know. If you put a plate in front of them and they say, "Yummy, I like this," and you say, "Ewww! It's not good for you." "Really?" The next time they are probably not going to like it as much, you know.

DB: But that enchantment is part of what poetry is most capable of and most beautiful at. The wisdom . . . what kind of wisdom does one derive from poetry?

WM: I read the other day that Jung as an old man said only a fool believes in wisdom. Of course we're all fools and there are archives of wisdom that we may come to. I think it's bred, that perspective, bred through sympathy.

We were talking about John Clare as we came up here. One of the wonderful things about Clare's poems is that he is more concerned with what he is writing about, whatever kind of creature it may be, he's right there, he is that creature, and it must be sort of a jolt to come back out of the pond for him.

DL: Talking about wisdom: In the poem you read to begin this session, what that's all about, it seems to me, is a transmission of wisdom across generations, a mother talking to her son about death and the afterlife and his remembering it many years later. But it's all an indirect kind of wisdom. Do you think that that's what poetic wisdom is about, an indirect kind of wisdom?

WM: The direct kind of wisdom would be commandments and things like that, I suppose, and I don't think that is wisdom in the same sense. I think the indirect kind of wisdom is the interesting one anyway. It's the thing, it's the question. The wisdom should probably take the form of a question that you can't answer.

DL: That's your Zen coming out.

WM: Oh, I don't know. I feel the same way about that that I feel about this whole matter of influence. What influences you? I don't know what influences me. Do you know what influences you?

DL: The Detroit Tigers.

WM: Everything I ever read, you know.

There is a woman who wrote a whole book, a small book, about me and Follain, Jean Follain, and how strongly influenced I had been by Jean Follain. She gave chapter and verse and went all the way back through everything. I wrote to her and said, "You know, you're using this as a doctoral thesis, I believe, and I think you better go over it more carefully because I didn't encounter anything of Jean Follain until I was past forty, and you're talking about things from my twenties and thirties." And then there was one poem, and it was a long time before I saw much more of Follain, and then, of course, I paid a lot of attention to Follain.

I think the important thing is affinity. And I think that finding things in various Eastern religions, religious traditions rather than dogmas, was more a discovery of an affinity. I mean, it was an articulation of something that I had been groping my way toward over the years, and I suddenly recognized it. And I think, you know, the affinity, that question of affinity, this is something that is both reassuring and academically troubling about the arts.

The arts are not about fulfilling some kind of academic obligation. They're about recognition. When you get something new, for example, when Beckett's first books came out, why was it that anybody understood them at all because there'd never been anything quite like it. The first readers who were excited by Beckett—and I number myself among them—were recognizing something that they had never encountered before. There it is already. You have that exciting paradox. You've never seen it before and yet you recognize it.

What does that tell us about us? I think that, you know, if we're encouraged to think of the arts as decoration—well, I don't think the arts are decoration. I think the arts are about the core things that our experience can't finally ever grasp, which is why the arts continue, you know, the way we continue.

DB: That's the fundamental trope in your poems, if I have to make that kind of long-reaching summary. It is not just the recognition of but embracement of paradox, of things in argument with each other.

WM: Yes.

DB: I mean, in your poems, paradoxes like these: the desire for home and the necessity for migration; the desire to articulate, yet the inevitable erasure or evasion of any kind of articulate finish or conclusion.

It seems to me that tension, more than anything else in your poems, shows us how to live, comfortably or uncomfortably, or how to live with that paradox of being in several places at once and accepting that as the human condition. That's one of the things that makes scholars so nervous. Who won? The answer must be either *this* or *that*. But the poet says the answer is always "all of the above."

I think when I first fell in love with your poems in college, I think it was that very recognition of an affinity—of being able to be in two places at once or to be comfortable with these opposite forces. It's the thing that gives such drama to your poems as well, I think. Maybe more than anything else.

WM: It's lovely, Dave.

DB: Well, I hope you recognize that. I think that's it.

So, let me ask you a question about being the poet laureate. I want to see if you are thinking about any projects that you have in mind for this position. I know that some of the laureates had public projects. Billy Collins had the Poetry 180 program and work he did in high schools. Kay Ryan has been doing things in community colleges. And Robert Pinsky started that wonderful and ongoing Favorite Poem project. I wonder if you had a project or a way to see this as an opportunity for a platform of something that you'd like to do.

WM: I haven't. I mean, I have thought about that, but I haven't gotten very far with it. For one thing, I live in Hawaii, and I don't want to make a lot of trips to the mainland, to the benighted states, as I call them, to do things like that. I have always, when asked if I possibly could, gone to grade schools and to other groups that are involved in conservation projects or dealing with animals or anything like that, and talked *with* them rather than *to* them, and I've enjoyed doing it. I've always learned something and they have, too.

I also go into prisons. I've gone to a number of prisons, and sometimes over a period of time have gotten to know some prisoners. I find that very satisfying.

I'm not someone who is very good about making up some kind of program. But I would welcome those (if it didn't involve extra trips from Hawaii)—I mean, there are a number of such things planned for the coming month. That is as near to a program as I may get.

But just talking about some of the things we were talking about a minute ago, that subject, which is I think not a simple subject. It's about a different way of looking at the world than the one that we are accustomed to, the very limited way that our society encourages us to think of as the only realistic way of considering it. It's not realistic if you're melting the poles and burning off the planet and killing another species every few seconds, and decreasing every few seconds your own chance of survival. I don't think that's very realistic.

So I don't think that the purely economic way of looking at the world is a very happy one. It's not a very respectful one. And I don't think it's very wise or realistic. It could be told that the arts are unrealistic.

DB: We're being told that often, now, aren't we? Unrealistic and unprofitable, and whole programs being cut from universities.

WM: And inconvenient.

DB: Inconvenient. Right.

DL: So, is poetry a way of looking at the world differently? Is it a route or a way to see the world from a different angle than the one you're talking about?

WM: I think it's a way of looking at the world for the first time. Don't you feel that every time you . . .

DB: That's very Emersonian.

WM: You recognize that. Emerson wasn't the first person to see it.

DB: Plato, I think. It is about, or your poems are about, again, a return to or a recollection of that primitive or primal or aboriginal moment of vision or insight, and the word that then comes to the mouth from such an awakening.

WM: Well, as I just said, in the arts, whether it's Beckett or Vermeer or Schubert, or whatever it is, there is the element of recognition that makes this connection, that makes the life between us.

But if you're asked what you recognize, the critics try to describe it, but we know that—without demeaning critics, I don't mean it that way—criticism is incapable of saying what it is that we are recognizing. They can talk all around it, but what is it that you are recognizing? I don't know. Can anybody say? Would you like to say what it is that you recognize when you saw *Waiting for Godot* the first time?

DB: Again, I think that's one of the fundamental questions of your poems. What you are doing is pointing at something that doesn't have a language, that doesn't have a word, and trying to accumulate a language that is as close as we can get to that inarticulable thing. That's one of the tensions that works in your poems over and over and over.

WM: But, you know, when David Lynn asked whether this was an influence from Eastern religion or anything of the kind, I don't know the answer to that. I know that, for example, as a very small child before I could read, I realized that there were things that I was feeling, things that I was seeing, and things I even thought I was thinking, that I couldn't express at all and will probably never be able to express.

I think everyone has that, has all that, and it's a precious thing to have. That is what we really are. And we should not let it be trashed or demeaned or shoved aside. And that's not part of the economic relation. That is not something that can be bought or sold.

You know, one's intelligence can be bought and sold. And one's knowledge can be bought and sold. All of those things. But that, that other aspect of each one of us, cannot be bought and sold. And I didn't have to discover or to start reading Eastern religions to come to that. I mean, that was there when I was sitting in church listening to "God the Father Almighty."

DB: How can that recognition be better nurtured in schools?

WM: I think that having teachers—you know—I think a huge bit of that is one on one. I think the arts work one on one. When somebody hears Schubert, only one person is hearing Schubert. There's a marvelous poem of Tomas Transtromer, who is a great Swedish poet who is still alive—

Yesterday we came in over the Triborough Bridge, which is the way that I like to come in to Manhattan, and I said to Paula, "Now, look. Look right now. Look down the river." And you look down and get the whole skyline of Manhattan. For years that had two towers at the end of it, too. But I remember from before the two towers, and Transtromer's poem is before the two towers, and he says, "This is the rim of the galaxy" that he is looking at. He's looking at it at night. He sees this whole thing and he says, "Each one of those windows, behind each of those windows, there is someone moving," which was true then.

It was before the World Trade Center was built and they left the lights on all night and there was nobody there. But he said, "In one of those windows there is a coffee cup on a table, and Schubert is playing." And he said, "To the person behind that window, nothing in the world is as real as Schubert."

DB: That's lovely, and true, that mystery.

DL: As we come to the end of this conversation, I wonder if you could share another poem with us from the set published in the new issue of the *Kenyon Review.*

WM: I would love to.

DB: We were suggesting "Homecoming?"

DL: "Homecoming" would be good. I think we've got a copy of that.

DB: I also love that little one right there.

WM: "By the Front Door"?

DB: Yes.

WM: There have been a number of little ones recently.

DB: Oh, that's nice!

WM: The little one you are talking about is "By the Front Door."

> Rain through the morning
> and in the long pool an old toad singing
> happiness old as water

DB: I love that one. It's connected to those Asian figures you were translating and "figuring" so many years ago. The poem that's almost not a poem, it's so irreducible.

WM: I've been working with a Japanese woman translator-friend. She does instantaneous translations, Japanese to English, for the United Nations. She is very, very good. We've done some modern poets, and for ten years we've been fooling around with Buson. I think Robert Hass did some Buson, too. I'll have to get his to make sure we don't overlap too much. But there's one I cited in Washington when I got there. It's in one of his series about cuckoos. It is the same cuckoo as the European cuckoo:

> In vain I listen for the voice of the cuckoo in the sky above the
>   Capitol.

DB: That one. That's wonderful.

DL: I almost feel that way today.

WM: Here is "Homecoming":

> Once only when the summer
> was nearly over and my own
> hair had been white as the day's clouds
> for more years than I was counting
> I stood by the garden at evening, same stanza
> Paula was still weeding around
> flowers that open after dark
> and I looked up to the clear sky
> and saw the new moon and at that
> moment from behind me a band
> of dark birds and then another
> after it flying in silence
> long curving wings hardly moving
> the plovers just in from the sea
> and the flight clear from Alaska

half their weight gone to get them home
but home now arriving without
a sound as it rose to meet them

DB: What a beautiful poem.

WM: Wittgenstein is supposed to have said—I've not been able to find where the quote came from, but somebody showed it to me—"Every poet who remains a poet beyond adolescence finds the true theme is homecoming."

DL: I love that sense at the end of the earth rising to meet the birds. It's an amazing closure.

DB: And it is a homecoming.

WM: I don't know what you know about plovers, but I love plovers. They're one of the reasons I wanted to have that piece of land there.

DB: They're in a lot of your poems.

WM: They are wonderful birds. After curlews, they are the great migrants. You could hear them, all through the summer there, all through the winter there, you could hear those two notes. Those two notes carry all through the horizon going across the sea. I looked up and said, "Those look like plovers, but they can't be plovers because I've never heard silent plovers." And I thought, "They're home! They're exhausted."

There was nothing to make a sound about. It was just fabulous.

Alice
Notley

MATT VALENTINE

ALICE NOTLEY has been one of the most prolific and adventurous of American poets for the past forty years. Born in Bisbee, Arizona, in 1945, and raised in Needles, California, she received her B.A. from Barnard College in 1967 and her M.F.A. in 1969 from the Writers' Workshop at the University of Iowa. In the 1970s and 1980s, she was a vibrant member of the Chicago and New York poetry scenes, and since 1992 she has lived and worked in Paris.

Alice Notley is the author of more than twenty volumes of poetry, beginning in 1971 with *165 Meeting House Lane* ("C" Press) and including, most recently, her award-winning collection *Grave of Light: New and Selected Poems 1970–2005* (Wesleyan University Press), *In the Pines* (Penguin, 2007), *Reason and Other Women* (Chax Press, 2010), and *Culture of One* (Penguin, 2011). A gathering of her essays and articles on poetry and poets, *Coming After,* was published in 2005 by the University of Michigan Press. Her work has been honored with a number of prizes including the Los Angeles Times Book Award for Poetry, an award from the American Academy of Arts and Letters, and the Shelley Memorial Award from the Poetry Society of America. She has been a finalist for the Pulitzer Prize, and in 2007 received the Lenore Marshall Poetry Prize from the Academy of American Poets for *Grave of Light*.

Notley's poetry takes many shapes and forms, from intensely personal poems to political narratives, from an experimental vigor to traditional lyricism. Like others of the New York School, Notley often crafts her poems as visual evocations, sifting her words across the page, sorting and decentering her phrases, and treating language as artistic material as much as a vehicle for the transfer of cognitive meaning. "It's necessary," she has said, "to maintain a state of disobedience against . . . everything."

When You Arrived

The immigrants arrive, grave and with torches, a billion of us.
In dreams you're compelled to be in the drama you're in.
I was sleeping with him at his desk, each had our own greyhound
His desk was a bed, the dogs were asleep at our flanks.
O savage and tender achings. The immigrants
mean to escape his parchment breakfasts,
his rococco edicts, his bloody fingertips. I left
because I was sad. I thought, What part of the world can't
be mine? I am an earthling, aren't I?
Why can't I live anywhere? The immigrants
try to escape their hellhounds; side effects are unclenched.
I have the identity of wrath. Where does it come from?
I am unconsolable under water, under your ugly armature.
We need protection and soldiers—oh no we had those at home
it doesn't work, we are roaming the globe to get away;
they keep coming after, plastic cops
not smart enough to be bitter, or sit down with their dogs
and smoke. No immigrant makes sense; I don't—
I wasn't born to make sense. I remember a corpse without interest
I am the living present no one knows. No one greets
Welcome to the living present, to your infidelity to the past
I'm adorned with my nightmares to please you: what else
would I have? You once did this too, remember?
When there were no maps and you walked changing everything
This trauma kept in a medicine cabinet: I heal myself with it
I use my motion to correct my regret: I open the
motion to behold you, send postcards, play the tune
of bravado. I rub motion on all my wounds.
Is no one in love with me? Billion immigrants have
each other. What will we do with our mirrors blackened in fire?

Attila the Gypsy Shakes Her Cup

Our connected wisdom, I was trying to hear, and speak,
our collective knowledge. I am experiencing déja-vu

Does it come in waves of thought or action?

You are not well-dressed enough. To enter the restaurant tonight, carrying
a plank on your head, like a surfboard.

My friends, we say, thirteen hundred immigrants arrived in Grand
          Canary last weekend.
I have inscribed this fact on my board.

The words you speak must be clear in their savage love of others,
all others; for we are one person, not understanding each other.

A common mouth. The young woman pressed her finger
above my left brow to let me, Wisdom, out. I hope to have a lot of
          disguises
and tongues. I am experiencing a frightening déja-vu.

I'm most afraid of the Room of the Gears. Someone else there in Control
Is it one of you? What's in control of each of us?
What I see, dream, speak, stands in for something else.
Credibly one will arrive at reality through the tunnel of these words.
I believe we will drink the cobalt water of truth
Then what of our intimacy? Truth
can be called, The Love of Strangers for Each Other.

Because I had already been in this time and was in it again,
I thought I was timeless. If you are, you experience the same time
          always,
in shock waves. There's someone inside you another you.
This is the City of Truth, it doesn't know what it's up to.

At some point I realized that I too was an immigrant;
Your Wisdom has been absent: I've come back.
Everyone is ravenous and on hunger strike. I'll sit down with you if you
     like.
I'm supposed to hold this moment together.

Hotel Truth Room

I am tough and sensible the older man said
Let's look at the map again.
I don't think we want it now—Look where it's taken us,
Democrat or Republican. Jealousy would make an interesting
film, not sexual jealousy
but the way a woman doesn't want another one to succeed.
Is this a poem? he asked. Do I have to be in it? I
need to find you to let you go. He said,
I thought you were jealous of my fame.
Sometimes, I say, I just want to be you—it's different.
Do you really think poetry is more important than film?
I don't think that way though I don't give a shit about

film. You look at me and see nothing but a movie.
You're too old to be in the film he said. So why are you
talking to me? You summoned me here. But you
own the room. There's so much light in here that I can't see you.
What do you want from me? Words.

The room is full of ghosts for a moment ghosts of live immigrants
looking for space to breathe in. You are all me but I'm having
a private moment. One says at night it's so
dark when I sleep I don't dream.

More urgency the film-maker said we really need that
his face is lined with his events, which I don't want to know
I don't want to know my own, except possibly from now.
The immigrants have trouble adorning themselves for each
other, when they live in squats. But they do it
Playing this beautiful instrument you can't see, a carved drum.

But they're not in the room he says. He smiles
You used to be blond, I say. We are uncovering
connections, standing by the window. I'm wearing
a necklace of dream-catcher baskets small and ornamental.

To Frank

These are my wartime experiences, that no one has considered
Occurring while one reads my poetry, as I am dead.
The pacific war pacified no one, and that's not my face,
on the figure in mind, grimed with tropical combat.
It's the cover of an edition of The Naked and the Dead.

I don't want to talk. Their piquant questions are too scholarly
for one who's chatting with her gynecologist over the stirrups.
Nude as a nut I told her I had two new books of poetry out
"How are they being received?"she asks and then that I grip her finger
with my vaginal muscles, "in case of leaks."

The layers of war come to order and proclaim themselves discernible
each decade with its enemies, mustard and wasabe, signifiers and
                confession
whatever that is, a faked statement after torture. They snag us
in their roaring gears; no one in Your generation has ever killed a person
It breaks the body to push out babies, I got red stars all over my chest
Some of the immigrants, machete users at age twelve,
won't make it. The Union's too unwieldy, we can't recognize
any more faces as our own—fact is we don't know How to be human.

The poet watches a grenade explode; I'm communicating with the
dead again it makes the gears go crazy I have just undergone
a bonafide 1970s panic attack; the poet was already dead by then
and I never met him anyway. Panic also temporarily
discombobulates the gears. I might die but maybe
I'll just give the perceptual frame a good whack
The poet tells me there's a real problem with the human person
it can't cope with its genius the poetic for an example an
extraordinary art delineating our being as it's lived, no one listens he
                says not
even my best friends, I have to fight *them*. The world is at war with
                poetry
he says, never smiling, beneath the ludicrous green netted helmet.

I'm adrift from my goals at last, winning the war
They were purposefully stupid then tugged at you
You've always been nice after all. He play-acted,
couldn't stand it; the way you write only one war novel
Because it continues. My birthday's full of dust I'm going to throw
on the machine. He's always been a part of me hasn't he
In the back room we two are creating an international culture of the
          ancient word.

We Have to Know How to Make the New One

Perhaps we had no reason to leave the previous continent but we left
we walked most of the way: it's what we do best; we also rowed
where the ocean was flat. Later, we always dreamed of this map
this pseudo beginning, doubting it. The newspapers said
we had journeyed more within our species or bodies, as stilly as
those illustrations of ape to man. Ah man! like a frosted cannoli.

We went down into the basement apartment, a confusing number
of people, lying around on the bed. There's a baby, neglected
who belongs to us; we are abandoning him; no we will feed
and take care of him; we will not have a huge head swollen-
looking aching with our ego, ourselves that cannot face
poetry's night and day, its high fair hills where no prizes grow.

For we have to know how to make the new one. And if the earth
cracks with drought we'll still have to. A strange wrinkled
ancestor hands us a nugget.

We must
keep changing our secret; it has to do it itself, secretly.
All night we've written our dialogue with a character named Ric
Ric says, for example, what we see is in light, isn't it? Or is it called we?
Then we find our orchestra in a restaurant; the oboist always says I, why?
In fact my pronoun is ever unassigned; we love us,
we kiss us, we make love to our astute and textured bodies
we tell us we will love us and remember us forever.

In the gray light they look worse and worse. With lined foreheads sit
and drink their lemon cokes. They wear three-piece suits, a fur stole;
they get in a car, for they're driving off to be shot. They have
flirted with danger and soon stand before the assembly
of golden filaments, nothing but shreds of what was.
You can't make us change. But I have changed and I am you
I am feeding the baby, I am telling the story, I am showing you
something, showing us something.

Someone is obsessively spanking the baby in a cave. Who, us?

Who are you speaking to? Where are you going? Who
bears the weight of our awakening?

Evident Being

A Conversation with Alice Notley

David Baker: These are five splendid poems, individually and as a gathering, Alice. We are glad for the opportunity to print them in the *Kenyon Review* and, in fact, for the chance to publish you for the first time in the magazine. I'd also like to talk more widely about your work, newer and older, and to range further into other subjects. I'm eager to find out about your view of American poetry from afar these days, and hear about works in progress, and maybe ask about your sense of the future of poetry and the arts.

But let's start with "We Have to Know How to Make the New One." This is one of my favorite new poems of yours. I have a few specific questions about it, but I wonder if there's anything you wish to say about it first—about its origin or impetus or whatever you might wish to say to begin.

Alice Notley: I wrote these poems in 2006; they're part of a larger group and so it's difficult for me to remember their individual geneses. I know that this one contains fragments of several dreams, but some aspects of it that sound like dreams aren't. I dreamed about a baby, I dreamed about an oboist I used to know. I dreamed the gangster-and-moll prelude to a shootout but not the "assembly of golden filaments." I think the poem is largely generated from previous poems in the manuscript, their themes and techniques. I had achieved a certain fluidity, an ability to travel across multiple subjects and scenes in a compressed way, to make certain unexpected but reasonable-sounding transitions. Suddenly I seemed to be saying what I had always been leading up to. I was able to assert things about our species inter-identification, about "I and we," and about my own sense that I had changed.

DB: Species inter-identification is a tantalizing term. I take this to mean something about a person's sense of connection with others, all the others. I'd like to come back to this in a minute, in fact. It seems to be related to the transfer of a singular to plural voice in this poem.

I'm also drawn to the end of this poem. The "weight" of those inter-rogatives at the end is very powerful. Over and over your poems are intended to provoke a method of "awakening." It is a long wait—to enjoy the pun—to arrive at a beginning.

In your essay, "Women and Poetry," you ask that very question: "What is it like at the beginning of the world?" Yet the title of your book of essays is *Coming After.* Do you think of your poems as searching for that beginning, or is the beginning always a belated one, an after-effect?

AN: I think I try with my poems to create a beginning space. I always seem to be erasing and starting over, rather than picking up where I left off, even if I wind up taking up the same themes. This is probably one reason why I change form and style so much, out of a desire to find a new beginning, which is always the true beginning. After a couple of people dear to me died in the eighties, I read a lot of books by Mircea Eliade that asserted that the response of indigenous peoples to any crisis was to recite their creation stories, to sing the world into being once more, but each time being always the first time. I seem to have incorporated this idea into my own procedures. But I'm always, also, trying to find out what really happened at the beginning. I don't accept any of the stories I know, though I find some of them quite interesting: I'm looking for my own, true version. And I'm looking for the perfect singing of it, the exact and perfect rendering. Of course a beginning can be a later one too, an *in medias res* beginning: it's something like, This is the beginning of my great change, my truest becoming, my deepest understanding of the world. This is what is really going on.

DB: I think you are referring to the death of Ted Berrigan, in 1983. So, in part, the crisis of this loss led you to creation stories?

That really is part of the sense I get in these five poems. They feel to me like a condensed saga, a kind of cultural history told with lyric com-pression. As a group, they begin with immigration and settlement, then sift through nightmare and war as well as smaller personalizing moments. And they lead, as we just observed, to questions. It's especially telling to see that the poems also amass from a singular first-person speaker toward a plural one—the "I and we" you mentioned earlier.

AN: This is perversely the result of my living in such intense solitude in Paris. I am quite isolated here, though when I visit the States I am probably too social. Here I am mostly alone, in my apartment, a condition that at first implies an extreme condition of "I" but somehow winds up as a "we." I cannot be French, but am I really American or anything at all except a member of the human species? Somehow my isolation reaches out towards the largest groupings. Partly because I have to bypass "clubs"— aesthetic groups and so on, people joined by similar opinions and habits.

As to your question about Ted, I think it was more the two later deaths that led me to creation myths and to epic, those of my stepdaughter, Kate Berrigan, and of my brother, Albert Notley Jr. It was particularly his death, bound up as it was with the Vietnam War, which pushed me into the world of *The Descent of Alette,* that subway full of despair and the impetus to create from it that I happened upon.

It's probably appropriate to say here that the "I" of Alette is explicitly a plural for the entire second book. Alette incorporates the personas of all the people in the subway into her own, becoming a blur of corporeal entities, which then leave her at the beginning of the third book. It is only as a one-person "I" that stands for "we" that she can take on the knowledge offered in the caves. I am still, twenty years later, trying to understand our given pronouns and my relation to them.

DB: So what are the difficulties or the vexations of speaking in the plural? What are the opportunities? I guess I'm thinking of the lyric's tendency toward the "I" as the speaking or singing self. Here, at least in this selection of five poems, the work assumes a collective experience. Is this then the tale of the tribe?

AN: Probably it is. I have, after seventeen years in Paris, come to the conclusion I live here. I am, as I say in one of the poems, an immigrant. That is one of my "we's." But, as I also say, there are millions, a billion of us. We are desperate and resourceful. We are cynical and hopeful. I am not willing to die to be here, as many immigrants are, but I can't imagine going back: who can ever imagine Going Back, like going back in time? One is too different, changed, ever to do that.

DB: You moved to Paris in 1992. Was this a reaction to American culture and politics? You have said in a past interview that "American politics are obviously upsetting and repellant. It's more and more outrageous each day." Are you in any way encouraged by recent developments, or do you continue with your dismay? Are you planning to stay in Paris?

AN: That I live here is mostly by chance—or by secret, magical design on the part of some force—as is everything in my life except maybe my poems. I came here with Doug Oliver, for personal reasons that had nothing to do with politics. Then he died of cancer, in 2000, and two years later, as I was beginning to feel more stable emotionally, I was diagnosed with hepatitis C. It was necessary for me to do a grueling eleven-month treatment. I remain here, where I have health care and an apartment. I have very little income, but maybe that doesn't matter. It doesn't really seem feasible for me to return to the States.

As for politics, I am not in the least encouraged by recent developments. Between 2001 and 2003 I wrote a book, *Alma, or The Dead Women* (published in 2006), that is motivated by grief for Doug's death and for all the deaths on 9/11 and in the subsequent bombing of Afghanistan, anticipating further deaths in Iraq. I find, after eight years, that we are still in Afghanistan bombing civilians, as well as bombing in Pakistan. We are, in fact, stepping up our activities, naming this war the "good one" or "right one." If I had the same kind of personal, grief-compelled energy as in 2001, I would probably write another 350-page book, denouncing the Obama administration rather than Bush and Cheney.

I am a pacifist, and I accuse my friends of being superficial pacifists trailing infatuated after a self-infatuated president. I refuse to allow my brother's own despair and death to be for nothing.

However I'm now ready for a change of tone of voice here!

DB: Okay, let's turn back to the tactic of these poems, the exchange of "I and we."

AN: When I wrote these poems I was reading John Ashbery's last four or five books. He uses "we" in an interesting way that he acquired from Auden but made different. Auden always seemed to be referring to his group of acquaintances or to his generation, which he was chiding towards and part of. But Ashbery, at least in my conception of Ashbery, can use "we" as if he is too weird to offer up his "I" to anyone as a point of identification. He isn't like anyone, but on the other hand he is like everyone. I can go with that usage, or my conception of it. More often Ashbery uses "I" but slides to a social "we"—no cowardly "they's"!

DB: Ashbery's a good case, isn't he? Vernon Shetley writes that Ashbery's difficulty grows out of his critique of the habits spawned by New Criticism —that is, his difficulty and his tactic of constant deferral as "a systematic negation" of the institutionalized methods of New Criticism. Ashbery simply refuses to hold still, in his scenes, his narratives, even his "voice."

But to me, his voice is quite different from yours. He evades where you reveal. Each of these five poems shows that. The voice here, as in "When You Arrived," may be made of pieces, memories, rediscovered phrases, but the sense of personhood is coherent and powerful.

AN: Well, as I say, I'm alone, and that seems to make my personhood more urgent.

Ashbery's pronouns are usually fictitious—he did his graduate work on Henry Green and Raymond Roussel, after all. By becoming someone else, he can go to those shimmery, unforeseen places that he wants to get to. I myself first studied at Iowa in the Fiction Workshop and have a strong grounding, too, in making things up.

In "When You Arrived," as an example, there is no content that is literally "true" or "real" that refers to me, except insofar as I am an immigrant, and some people would contest that and opt for something like "expat." Though every ten years I must stand in line outside a building for hours and hours in order to have my papers renewed. I am, in this poem, identifying with Africans and Asians and Arabs, all the people I stood in line with in 2002. The Southern Hemisphere especially is in an active state of upheaval, with people moving upward, escaping brutal governments, global warming scenarios, or pennilessness, as everyone in the southwestern United States knows well.

DB: The notion of voice is complex, isn't it? Your own essay entitled "Voice" has helped me think through some things. I hear young poets talk about wanting to establish their voice. I know what they mean, I think, though they tend to confuse voice with authority or with—this is even worse—a kind of marketable entity, a trademark.

I tend to think that voice is something we achieve or can identify rather long after the fact.

AN: I never devoted much thought to voice until the late eighties and nineties, when the voice seemed to become suspect, as if selfish or old-fashioned, rather than the undeniable fact of poetry that I think it is. In fact, voice was the one thing I had identifiably from the beginning of my poethood. I can hear myself practicing for my first poetry reading in 1970, when I had very few poems, and realizing that I had something like "a voice"—without thinking that phrase. It was some sort of sound glue, it was electrical, and I truly possessed it, but not much else at that time.

For me the concept is bound up with poetry readings, reading aloud, listening to recordings of dead poets. Every poet, even those considered poor readers, reads her or his own poems better than actors do, who are invariably horrible readers (though they don't think they are). Voice is bound up with that quality that makes the poet that better reader.

DB: How is a poetic voice connected with the concept of self or personhood? You touched on this a minute ago in discussing the literally "true" content of a poet in relation both to the speaking self of that poem and to the autobiographic self.

This is all a vexation for me, I confess. Some people regard self as a trope only, a fiction that helps us, at least, perpetuate the species. Others see a self as a stable fixed entity, while others see self as entirely diffuse. You talk about voice as an achievement of "unity." Can you say more?

AN: "Self" is a really clunky, meaningless word now. No one ever bothers to define it for fear of sliding in muck and having to say "soul" or something. I had first thought of it as Yeats does in "A Dialogue of Self and Soul," but the newer usages of the word seemed to lump the two together in order snottily to erase both. A friend told me, after I prodded him mercilessly, that what is meant is really soul, but I think he meant with tinges of self.

At some point I decided I liked the use of "self" in the sense of Atman in the Hindu Upanishads—the most basic entity isolatable, stripped-awayable-to in meditation. In one of the Upanishads it's said that you can envision it as a little thumb. So please now tell everyone that the self is a little thumb! I also like to think of it as poverty, as I say in my poem "Lady Poverty" in *Mysteries of Small Houses*. But then I obviously mean "soul" more than "self." Self strips away to soul but then is it. The poetic voice knows this even if it's a hugely socialized voice. I might add that the poet doesn't always know what her voice or poem knows. The voice is comprised of what is most individual about the poet, the poet's physiology, temperament, background, plus the poet's understanding and talent. It's what we work with, really. For we are talented in the way musicians and painters are, working with specifics that only we, the talented in poetry, know how to manipulate. We have an ear for very fine changes of sound and meaning between letters and words and lines.

DB: You have said all along that you have wanted to write an epic—as you have written—a female epic. And some of your poetry has the sweep and broken grandeur of epic. I'm thinking of *The Descent of Alette,* for instance, with its accumulating scraps of language-as-citation, or *Beginning with a Stain,* among others.

Do you see these five poems as a kind of mini-epic? Certainly there's an impulse toward history-making here, or history-telling, and touches of other aspects of an epic narrative.

AN: These poems are part of a group of forty or more poems called *My City.* When I selected these five I noticed they did stick together rather epically, and I wondered if I needed the rest of the poems. However I seem to be able to group the other poems rather interestingly too, in fours and fives. What I can't seem to do is finish the manuscript. I have actually completed a sixty-five-page poem taking off on the two characters in "Hotel Truth Room," but I can't quite complete this sequence. I'm almost there though.

DB: Are you at work on any other poetry that has epic aspirations?

AN: I have a lot of manuscripts lying around, most of which are long narratives. The one I just referred to, involving the filmmaker and the poet, is called *Eurynome's Sandals*. The poet is now Eurynome, who in the Pelasgian creation myth danced the world into being; the filmmaker becomes the cosmic serpent, whom I identify with Time. There's an earlier poem called *Negativity's Kiss*, which I have excerpted from in a lot of poetry journals, which is also a straight narrative. Well, not that straight. A rather hybrid work called *Songs and Stories of the Ghouls*—hybrid between poetry and prose and likewise pretty narrative—will be published by Wesleyan in the future. And yet another narrative work called *Culture of One* is to be published next by Penguin. The five poems *Kenyon* has published are different in that they point to narrative and epic but are part of a more "lyric" project. I can't always tell the difference between narrative and lyric, epic and lyric, I just write the stuff; but I seem to have developed a strong storytelling instinct over the years.

DB: Well, that's a lot of new work! I'm already looking forward to seeing these.

I can't often tell the difference between narrative and lyric, either. With epic I expect some centralized sweep of history, a larger-than-one-person concern. I tend to look at lyric and narrative, however, as points on a continuum rather than either/or modes. All poetry ought to have lyric traits, don't you think? And language itself—even that most basic handoff of subject and predicate—is narrative, tracing the passage of time or event or linguistic exchange.

Your poem "Hotel Truth Room," for example, gives a wonderful and wild set of associations, the kinds of leaps of imagination I think of as lyric. Yet there is a central story, or a central pattern of narratives connected by this voice and this "room." Part of the story is, again, that relation between the "private moment" of a lyric voice and the collective imagination or force of others, "Democratic or Republican." "You are all me," the "I" here says.

AN: The "You are all me" stanza seems very private and personal, as if the "I" in the poem has changed from being a character in a dialogue to the poet herself. But the two speakers in general are more fictionalized than that "I," aren't they? And stand for things beyond themselves, men and women, the subjugation of women to men. But also the subjugation of poetry to film, the relegation of it to a hotel-room-type space. The film-maker is there for sex, basically, if "for sex" means something more general than the act.

And now I'm recalling that one of the themes of *The Descent of Alette* is the need for the more worthy or moneyed classes—the tyrant and his—to get their art and their thrills in the more squalid places, among the people who are forced by circumstance to confront their emotions constantly—the artists by extension. Women, of course, are denigrated for their supposed emotionality; and I am sometimes charged with being "emotional."

DB: That turns me back to the other important factor in your phrase the "female epic." We have talked about epic, but what about the female part of that phrase? Will you say more about the distinguishing features of epic that you want to engender with female aspects?

AN: That was part of what I attempted in *The Descent of Alette*—I'm not consciously doing the same sort of thing now, though I've probably internalized it into my approach to the long poem. That is, I wanted to write a traditional epic and was baffled by the need in the form for masculine action, warriorly confrontation, the seizure of thrones and so on. I didn't feel interested in creating a female hero with martial arts skills, as in the comics, a babe who can kill. I also have problems with a description of time as story, though I will adhere to it to write certain kinds of works. I had been researching my dreams a lot, and it seemed that for me action was always stunted. The dream ended before the culminating, disastrous or triumphant blow, in fact tended to consist of single episodes that never went on. I later, in *Disobedience,* theorized time as consisting more of tableaux than of lengthy narrative.

Anyway, I found in the story of the Sumerian goddess Inanna, and her descent into the underworld, a prototype for Alette. Inanna shows up, she observes, she dies in fact, is reborn, but never fights. She makes certain crucial decisions, the most profound one being the decision to confront death by appearing at the door of the underworld. Alette, on the other hand, does fight, but the fight is magical and not bloody. It was very difficult for me to stage her fight with the tyrant, since I am a pacifist. But he is a construct, a symbol; she isn't.

DB: You hint at aspects of gender and prosody, too, in a question that comes up in "American Poetic Music at the Moment." You were talking in that essay about some early influences of yours—O'Hara and Whalen and Denby, for example—when you began to wonder, "How could a girl have a line?"

That's a delicious, loaded question. It suggests a manner of prosody, for one. Is there a kind of line that is female? It also suggests a line of work, a vocation. And perhaps even a subtle come-on. Care to expand on any of that?

AN: I know that certain people theorize a female way of writing, but I'm not really interested in that train of thought. What baffled me when I was young was the seeming assurance with which men took on a particular poetic line—long or Creeleyesque or Ashberyan or Objectivist—and stuck with it, as if something within them told them what their fated form was, or what the best way to write was. And the lines all seemed to belong to someone else already. As a woman I connected with no particular line, no way of writing.

I remember all the guys who were imitating Ashbery at the time. I kept asking everyone what the hell Ashbery was doing with his conjunctions, but no one ever answered me. Like true poets, they just did it without knowing what it was, by ear.

As I say in the essay, I finally arrived at a scheme for ending my line at the edge of the notebook page—I usually wrote by hand in rather wide, unlined notebooks. This way I threw the question back to its origins: What is a line? What was I doing using the line?

DB: Yes, I know that comment in the essay. As you say, you determined your length of line by the width of your notebook at the time. That reminds me of Dickinson filling each scrap of available paper, even writing down the side of a page, making use of what's there.

You mentioned earlier that you change form and style a lot. Your lines are sometimes huge, sometimes very slender, sometimes fragmented. In these five poems, the line is spacious but clearly not prose-like. Sometimes here you use punctuation at line's end, as the first two lines in "What You Arrived." And sometimes the line-end itself serves as sufficient punctuation, as in the third, which produces a kind of hastened syntax or even a jump-cut to another voice or scene.

I'm interested in how you perceive of line. As you have written, "Poetry is primarily the line." Could you say more?

AN: The line is an utterly malleable organizing principle influenced by all sorts of things but symbiotic with the language one speaks. French prosody, for example, is traditionally syllabic because there are no fixed accents in the spoken language. Latin and Greek prosodies are stressed based on vowel quantity, but the Romans were imitating the Greeks rather than their own language necessarily, which had originally provoked a stress-accented verse that nobody seems to know much about. English is stress-accented, but there are a lot of Englishes now; the traditional English lines won't do for a lot of Americans or modern Brits. So many languages are in flux, much more than they used to be, and it makes sense for poetry's most basic elements to be unfixed at the moment.

I have recently worked a lot in prose—which entails a very fluid, undercurrented sense of line—but am also doing things with Latin and Greek meters. As everyone knows you can't utilize them well in English, but you can do dances around them. I wouldn't dream of ever telling anyone exactly what I'm doing, it would sound too dopey, and I don't want anyone to know.

DB: Well, I'm completely curious about what you are doing with classical meters. I can't imagine what it might be, unless you are working in quantitative metrics, something with vowel duration or perhaps pitch. This is all nearly impossible in English, and most of the few examples I can call to mind are pretty awful. But I won't ask . . . unless you could be coerced into revealing.

AN: A few years ago I tried reading Horace out loud, keeping to the meter as it was presented in the abstract at the front of the Loeb Classics edition. I heard something I'd never heard before, a different possibility for cadence. It was the complexity of the line that was getting to me, something far removed from just going along boppity-bop or walky-walk, the way one often does, in free or unfree verse. The foot is more like one of my quotation-marked phrases in *The Descent of Alette* or like Williams's variable foot, but it's denser. Partly because of the quantitative aspect, but also because of how inflected the Latin is. I've been somewhat entranced ever since, but shyly, since I don't have a real classics education. Coincidentally, I'd just been contacted by my old high school Latin teacher; we corresponded and he sent me some lovely old books about prosody. All of this is what I think about at the moment when I want to have some official poetry thoughts.

DB: You speak so fully of sound, of the auditory aspects of poetry. Is a poetic line primarily auditory for you, or visual, or a breath-unit, or some other form of measurement and structure?

AN: It is primarily auditory, and even when I'm working in the territory of set meters, it becomes intuitive. However I'm interested in page layout, too. On that level I'm trying to score for the page, so the reader will know how to say the poem silently. I suppose I'm also trying to make the poem visually attractive; it's hard not to go there, and I have a lot of visual training from my interactions with painters and from my own collage-making.

DB: I wonder about your vantage of current American poetry as seen from abroad. What are you reading that excites you? Which younger poets seem interesting to you?

AN: I'm afraid I'm mostly reading the ancients right now, plus my usual crime novels and history books. I of course read my sons' new books and manuscripts and keep track of what their friends are doing. I don't want to name people for fear of exclusion of someone—I don't want any of these ones mad at me, they're still too dear. But young poets come to Paris, look me up and drink coffee with me and pick my brains. I adopt them on some level, and we keep in touch. It feels like I know hundreds of younger poets at this point. Though they're all getting older—but then more and even younger ones show up.

DB: What do you look for when you read new poetry? Are there particular qualities of innovation that you seek or find yourself most receptive to?

AN: Most innovation has as much to do with a change in tone of voice or of subject as it does with a change in style or diction. The appearance of schools like the Beats or New York School required a change of tone, didn't it? The appearance of so many women poets was a definite changing of the subject. When you change these aspects, you end up changing your style, your approach to the language, if you're any good. Most of the purely linguistic innovation possible must have been done by now. But I like a new kind of wordplay when it shows up, why not?

I guess I'm attracted a lot by tone of voice and by sheer athletic ability—vocabulary, pace, how line and syntax are being manipulated. I also look for information—what does this person know, in the sense of depth and observation? A quality of knowing can be conveyed in what might seem like very obscure poetry to some. Some writers give sheer sensuous pleasure using words a certain way, and I respond to that. There's also an esthetic honesty I like that's hard to describe, a sense that this is the only possible poem, formally, the poet could be writing at this moment.

DB: I read a lot of poetry by younger poets, too. I stay on the lookout for innovative poets. I also pay attention to the relationship between current poetry and critical theory.

Much of the poetry of the past thirty or forty years, especially Language and post-Language poetry, seems intimately tied to post-structural theory. But you seem to have resisted the theorizing of poetry.

AN: My coming-of-age as a poet predates the Language movement, and I haven't been influenced by the Language poets or by theory. Language poetry is derived from second-generation New York School poetry, with which I am often associated, fused with European theoretical sources and other sources. They got a lot of their techniques and methods from us. The Language poets and I do not claim each other, but we are friends. I'm just not interested in theory and never have been. And I certainly don't believe anyone ought to be writing in any particular way at a given time.

DB: I think I'll ask the question about young poets and theory, since these two forms of practice or discourse are the two biggest expressions of growth in American universities. Young poets are weaned on theory. Does this trouble you or encourage you? How comfortable should poetry be in the academy? How dependent on theory should poetry be?

AN: Theory has nothing whatsoever to do with poetry. The only thing that matters is how much talent someone has and how far they're willing to go with it—the rest of it's largely bullshit, though it's possible one needs some bullshit in life. But poetry should feel hugely uncomfortable in the academy. I say this realizing that poets need to make money, and I can't really advise anyone to live the way I do. I went to Iowa because I was trying to figure out how to be a writer; going there was the best thing I could possibly have done for myself at the time because I finally met other writers. But I didn't understand that the M.F.A .was a teaching degree—and there were only a couple of programs then. Where was one supposed to teach creative writing? I was shocked that I was expected to teach a class or two at Iowa and refused to, so they gave me some other work to do—they were admirably flexible. But so many people are attached to the programs now, a circumstance that creates an inbred conversation; everyone reflects each other like mirrors.

DB: It's been a great pleasure to trade these questions and answers with you, Alice.

One last question, for those young poets we were just discussing. What do you see as the work to be done now in poetry? What opportunities, or directions, do you see? I guess I'm asking: what next?

AN: It's all about the planet. Everyone's going to be trying to save the future. If we revert to stone-age conditions, there will still be poetry going on around the fires, but first we have to go through the motions of saving ourselves. I don't feel positive about any of this. I wrote a long poem "about" global warming in 1993 called *Désamère,* and when it was published no one even mentioned that that was what it was about, even though I was explicit, and explicit in the introduction to the book (which also contains the long work *Close to me & Closer . . . (The Language of Heaven))*.

No one's really facing up to this reality as the massive danger to us it is, but the poets could. It should be incorporated into the totality of what one says. I'm not talking about being didactic, I'm talking about knowing what's going on and showing that as part of one's evident being, one's work.

Meghan
O'Rourke

SARAH SCHATZ

MEGHAN O'ROURKE was born in 1976 in Brooklyn, New York, and grew up there. She earned her B.A. from Yale in 1997, and that summer began her literary career at the *New Yorker,* first as an editorial assistant, then in 2000 as an editor. Since 2002 she has served as culture editor for *Slate,* and in 2005 was named co-poetry editor of the *Paris Review* where she now serves as consulting poetry editor.

In April 2007, W. W. Norton published O'Rourke's first book of poetry, *Halflife,* which was followed in 2011 by *Once,* also from Norton. Readers will find individual poems of hers in the *New Yorker,* the *New Republic,* the *Yale Review,* the *New York Review of Books,* and her prose in *Poetry,* the *New York Times Book Review, Slate,* the *LA Times Book Review,* and elsewhere. Her cultural criticism ranges from topics in gender bias, film and popular fiction, and grieving, to the politics of marriage and divorce. In 2011 O'Rourke's bestselling memoir, *The Long Goodbye* (Riverhead Books), about the death of her mother from cancer, was published to wide critical acclaim.

115

O'Rourke's poetry is sophisticated but accessible—remarkably so, on both accounts, for someone so young. Readers will notice an impressive formal range, from short lyric poems—even haiku—to longer narrative and historical sequences. O'Rourke's poetry makes use of literary allusions and rich tropes and presents a wide historical range and cultural aptitude; but she is capable, too, of personal narratives that bear great tenderness and vulnerability. These are fairly uncommon traits in the work of younger and emerging American poets.

Winter Palace

By my hands I hang in the bedroom
of a man's strange mind.
The walls are lined with fleurs-de-lis
made from the fur of mice.
Smoke rises in the chimney.

Yet another plague—
in northern pastures long-nosed horses
stamp at the smell of bodies
burning behind the castle.
The rope around my fingers creaks,

moths bang against the window,
a doctor stumbles up the walk—
the corners are full of needles
to help me sleep,
mice lie like kings in their copper traps.

Keep still, he says,
the vein is hard to find
without a little pinch. See?
Supervision is so
much better than freedom.

The Lost Sister

She was a master of childhood, very green,
very given to play, very sleepy, very grit of gray.
I, I was a shadow in a tree for no one to see,
I was a piece of ice in a tidal sweep.
When she laughed the sea made order of disorder.
I was a shadow in a tree, a stain
along the thawing bough for no one to see.

In her life, the hours pass casually.
Snow continues to pile on snow,
the dust in the corners of the old farmhouse
grows like mice in the winter.
I, I was the snow that fell too soon,
before the ground had frozen enough to catch me
and make me stick.

Peep Show

Tokens in the slot:
ka-shot, shot, shot.
A figure in the darkness.
The tin crank
of canned do-wop.

Someone is always watching—
don't you think?
Duck, turn, and wink.
Bodies at a distance—
that's what we are,

raises, renovations, Florida,
dinner by the sea.
Look at you.
The waves go swiftly
out of sight—

a long ellipsis
of glaciers swallowing the sun—
come quick, no time for this,
the girls in thongs
are glancing at the clock.

Sandy Hook

The fire burned my cousin here.
First in his bed in the bungalow garage.
Then at the lock, scratching in fear.
Quick, quick. The trundle bed
burned. The violin, unpracticed, burned.
The keys of the body, burned. Yellow, red,
the turning leaves. The burning
thing, ablaze, a living shroud: smoke, air, bone,
a licking; then the carbonite no one looks at twice.
The instrument, delinquent with disuse.
Outside, the hooks of the waves twist
and desist, twist and insist,
like coats hung out beneath
the snailing clouds to dry.

War Lullaby

Wet daggers of grass
cast shadows over one another
beneath the porch light—

the boy stretched on the lawn,
fighting sleep,
fingers the tournament ring:

inside the house
his mother shouts, blinds
slap in the breeze,

and upstairs the smallest stir
as they sleep, eyelashes like
tiny whips against their cheeks.

The dogs bark, a door slams,
the boys breathe deep,
then shudder—

I have seen them
sleepwalk
out of the arms of mothers.

That Sensation of Privilege and Loss

A Conversation with Meghan O'Rourke

David Baker: Meghan, thank you for conducting this long-distance interview. I'd like to start our conversation with these five poems and then move outward toward your new book, *Halflife,* and to your other work as culture editor for *Slate,* poetry editor for the *Paris Review,* and critic of contemporary writing and culture.

I'm struck first of all, in all five of these poems, by the intensity and spareness of the language. Who are your models for your style? What are your aspirations for your individual poems, like these?

Meghan O'Rourke: Thanks for having me, David. These are great questions, and I'll do my best to answer them.

My models are always changing, it seems. When I was writing the poems that appear in the *Kenyon Review*—mostly in 2003—I had been reading William Carlos Williams, Sylvia Plath, Apollinaire, Wallace Stevens, and Louise Glück, among others. In one way, Plath was probably the most overt model. It took me a long time to be able to read Plath carefully; I had always been distracted by the impudence of her emotions, and the way the myth of the life overshadows the work. But as I read more carefully I saw how she was able to compress an awful lot of torque into a few short lines. Consider "Poppies in October." It starts out with the poet in a mode of amazement—"Even the sun-clouds this morning cannot manage such skirts," she says of the poppies. But the poem quickly becomes an exclamation of doubt: "Oh my god, what am I . . ." (You've got to love those monosyllables.) I was fascinated by the way the apparent demureness of the opening gave way to such bald intensity, and how the mechanics of the verse powered that.

But—especially as a young woman—you have to get away from Plath's influence. Wallace Stevens was a useful counter-point. *Harmonium* is reticent where *Ariel* is declarative. And reading Williams was crucial: his superb sense of line, his energy, his strange swerves. I wouldn't have written "War Lullaby" if I hadn't been reading Williams.

DB: Yes, I understand the need to absorb Plath and then get away from her. Glück, too, I think. Both are such strong stylists, with a kind of contagious power. Stevens and Williams are also interesting models in your case, since each wrote very long poems and short ones. Your own style, as you've noted, leans toward the latter—brevity, concision, the elliptical or elided, the intense and spare. What do you see as the virtues of intensity and spareness?

MO'R: You know, it's never occurred to me that intensity was anything but a virtue. For so long I have seen it as the primary quality of what language can do. Didn't Nietzsche once say that he wanted every sentence to explode? That's how I felt. As a reader or viewer, largely what I look for in literature, or art, or films, is an aesthetic experience so vivid that it becomes experience itself, a kind of high. Saturation, in film; the use of crescendo and decrescendo, in music; the messed-around-with brush stroke, in paintings. This may seem callow to me someday, but that's how it is now.

Spareness is another matter. I didn't actually consider spareness a virtue for many years; much of the poetry I loved was big: Walt Whitman, Frank O'Hara, John Ashbery, Anne Carson. When I was first writing the poems here I was actually trying to write BIG poems that overflowed the vessel in which they were contained. But I kept just producing work that explained too much. Finally, I began to see that the problem wasn't that the poems needed *more* but less. If the poem was a river, I had jump from log to log across it, rather than try to build imposing bridges. And so elision became pleasing. Space became pleasing.

DB: I'm also struck by the very powerful stance of the speaker in these poems. These are far from the typical personal-confessional speaker so common in our current poetry. There are intonations of earlier days—plagues and wars and glaciers—but of course these suggestions also resound with the plagues and wars of our moment. There are also landscapes here, suggestive of places beyond your New York home. How do you think about your stance, your speakers, the sites for your poems?

MO'R: I'm glad to hear that they don't seem personal. I never wanted to write autobiographical poems. For a long time, I was horrified by the idea of anything connected "literally" to my life. The details of my life seemed so . . . available. In my early twenties, I swore by Eliot's notion that the poem is not an expression of personality, but an escape from it, and I wrote vague, high-minded poems. This lack of clarity was not a virtue. Gradually I saw that the speakers of the poems did have to reveal what was at stake for them—even if it was not about *me*.

That's not to say that autobiography doesn't shape the work. I wrote these poems in the years after 9/11, and at the time I had the feeling that the world was coming to an end. I remember thinking that if I could just use the right words all the time, the world might become more durable. Many of the poems were about imagining my speakers into extreme places, and helping them find the language to express their dilemmas. I wanted to get beyond the self. To get there, it seemed to me, required a disciplined immersion in the imagination—a way of taking in everything I'd read, and capturing my own pleasure as a *reader* in not being limited to my historical moment. The intonations in the poems had to be layered, to convey that sense of the ribs of the past sticking through the skin of the present. They also had to move broadly through America, to capture its bigness, its plurality, its contradictions.

Fairy tales seemed particularly resonant as a method for creating tension. "Winter Palace" originally tried to reimagine the Bluebeard story: What if Bluebeard's wife married him *knowing* about all the dead wives? I got far away from this literal conceit, but that question—about subjecting yourself to someone with whom you are erotically obsessed—governed the poem. At the time of writing, there was still smoke blowing from the World Trade Center, or there recently had been; in any case, I was still haunted by the smell of the city burning. That crept into the poem, with the horses stomping their feet. Likewise, *real* plagues or disasters are exactly what you don't read about in fairy tales, which contain every other kind of horror and trauma you can imagine.

DB: Of these, "The Lost Sister" leans closest toward the "real" of the personal. It is also part of a longer sequence, I know. Can you say a little about that poem and the sequence?

MO'R: That sequence was suggested to me by the poet Ellen Bryant Voigt. It began as a series of distinct poems that I couldn't finish—poems that, for the first time, I felt I was transcribing rather than writing. For example, I had the opening of the one you're publishing ("She was very sleepy, she was very grit of grey"). I was attracted to the music. But when I tried to clarify who this speaker was, the voice died. Other fragments arrived; it became clear that in each there was a dead twin speaking to her living sister. But I couldn't find a way to make this information available to the readers without diluting the focus of the poems. Then Ellen read the fragments and suggested that they were part of a series: two sisters, one living, one dead, in dialogue—an option that would never have occurred to me, I don't think. As soon as she said that, I knew she was right. I went on to finish the series very quickly.

The one you're publishing is perhaps my favorite. It's a poem about memory and the interstitial quality of life when we are very young—how fragmented yet indelible our memories of that period are. It's from the point of view of a girl who never lived, but who felt closest to her living sister during her twin's first years of life. Of course, the dead sister also covets her living sister's ability to experience physical sensations for the first time.

DB: These five poems are included in your first book of poems, *Halflife*. You must be excited. I have enjoyed reading the whole manuscript very much. These five poems also seem to me representative of some central movements of the book—the intense and spare style, which we've noted, your capability to speak of personal issues but without the pandering or self-important stance that can infect contemporary poets, the oblique but central narrative of maturation—coming-of-age as a woman, as an artist and intellectual, a citizen. Can you talk a little about your own aspirations for the book?

MO'R: It is an oblique narrative, isn't it? I hope not too much so.

I suppose I can recognize my aspirations now, but while I was writing the book I felt like I was sleepwalking, going in search of something I couldn't see. I did know that I wanted to write about belief, about speakers who felt the pressures of postmodern irony and skepticism—the pressures of contingency—but who were, fundamentally, trying to hold on to something they thought was true. I also wanted to write poems that in some way ran counter to the governing therapeutic narratives of late-twentieth-century America—narratives of psychological redemption. Finally, my favorite literature has always been that which deals with the individual's search for truth, for transcendence, for spiritual peace outside of the conventions of society. And it interested me that this particular desire for transcendence, in Western literature, is strongly identified as a male quest. In such texts, in fact, the female almost always represents an obstacle to the protagonist's search—or, if not an obstacle, then at best an embodiment of his duties to society, of the routinization of his individuality. Think about Williams's poem "Danse Russe," in which the speaker exclaims, after his wife has gone to bed, "I am lonely, lonely. / I was born to be lonely, / I am best so!" I always found it confusing to figure out who I was in that poem—was I the speaker, who gleefully celebrates his solitude, or did I have to be the pragmatic wife sleeping downstairs? Women typically aren't sent on this kind of quest, and when they are, their sexuality always gets in the way. (Surely that's why Emily Dickinson was always hiding behind doors.) In some way, I wanted the book to tackle that tension, and to self-consciously comment on it.

DB: Yes, I know what you mean about the female-as-foil to the protagonist. Williams is a good example. I think just now of "The Young Housewife," that poem where he drives slowly by a house, imagines the lonely woman there as a leaf, then is aware of his running over fallen leaves in his car. So quietly brutalizing.

The issue of transcendence is fascinating, and as you say is typically gendered into a male quest or proof of power. Many of your poems in *Halflife* are committed to searching deeper into this world, though, the sensual realization of it. In "The Climber in the Ice," you insist, "This is how it is. / I can taste the rock, I mean, *taste it*. . . ." And in your *Kenyon* poems, the persisting gesture toward the poems' conclusions is of clarity and particularity, rather than the kind of blurring or erasing other-world-reaching we may regard as transcending. How much are you aware of those kinds of gestures? Do you find a value in the transcendental, or is it an antique trope, best assigned to the past?

MO'R: "The Climber in the Ice" is certainly about dealing with the earth-bound physicality of emotion, rather than with intimations of transcendence. It was inspired by reading of a mountain climber who'd been found in the ice many years after her death. I was interested in that trope —the mountain climber—with its Romantic resonances, and interested in how differently we think about grandeur today, as the product of serotonins, neurobiology, nodes of pleasure in the brain.

I feel fairly conscious of the gestures I make in the poems—at least after the fact!—but surely lots happens that I don't know about. It's true that many of the poems are committed to capturing the particularity of sensual experience, but it seems to me that others, such as the title poem, close with abstract, enlarging gestures. The final lines of the first poem in the book are "Look again, and up you may rise / to find something quite surprising in the distance," for example. These may not exactly be *blurring* gestures, or the traditional reaching after universals that denoted transcendence for both the English Romantics and American transcendentalists. Then again, as Emerson said, "There is no fact in nature which does not carry the whole sense of nature," and I suppose it's his fascination with the way that small facts can become great symbols—even of our intuitions of otherworldliness—that interested me when I was writing these poems. But in a sense that answers your second question: that for me, at least, the old tropes of transcendence do feel antique, which is not to say unusable, or irrelevant, or unimportant, only that we have to earn our usage of them and find new ways to convey our otherworldly intuitions. I suspect it has a lot to do with what one can write about with authority.

DB: Okay, authority, or authorship: How did you come to compose *Halflife?* Some poets write one poem at a time, and just gather them together at last and arrange them into a book. Some poets write with a sense of a book project, from the beginning. How did you put *Halflife* together?

MO'R: Ah, how I wish I was one of those poets who has a sense of the project from the beginning. The poems in this book date back to early 2002. But until late 2004, I was writing one poem at a time—or maybe, to put it more accurately, one suite of poems at a time. And I had several groups of what seemed to me to be really different work that couldn't be gathered into a coherent collection. At some point, though, I put them together and cut others and began to see threads of connection. (Ellen Bryant Voigt was again instrumental to this process.) Once that happened, I saw what needed to be filled in, and I began to work with more sense of purpose. I set myself a deadline of finishing in the fall of 2005. That forced me to be quite hard-headed about my time, and to become obsessed with the manuscript, so that I was continually shaping and reshaping it, looking for the larger frame that would house the individual poems.

DB: Then how did you know you were finished? That's not a trivial question, or problem. I talk to many poets—emerging and established—for whom the finishing of a book is nearly impossible. I may be one of those.

MO'R: It was odd. I had given myself an artificial deadline of November 1, because I usually can't put anything down unless I'm made to. One day in October, I printed out the manuscript to see how it read with some poems I'd just finished. After reading it, I thought: *I'm done.* I was surprised. It wasn't that I didn't see the book's flaws; but something about its shape told me I had gone as far as I could with it.

I did try to add work after Norton had accepted the book—about six or seven poems that seemed consonant with the project. But it was as if

I'd put too many plants in a room with no windows: all the oxygen got sucked out. I had to take most of the poems back out. Of course, I have made some tweaks, but mostly in poems that I knew were still settling into their shapes.

DB: Our readers may know you for your other work, too. You've been the culture editor of *Slate* for several years, and have more recently been appointed as co-poetry editor, with Charles Simic first and now with Dan Chaisson, of the *Paris Review*. First, how do you find the time?

MO'R: Not sleeping? I did have insomnia for a while, which helped. In all seriousness, I have a great staff at *Slate,* and I've been able to scale back to four days a week there. The *Paris Review* also has a wonderful group of readers, who help out tremendously. Even so, the poems go to both me and my co-poetry editor—who's also quite busy—so we're too slow about getting back to people.

As for my own writing, my father once gave me some good advice. He wrote his Ph.D. dissertation while holding two jobs and raising three kids with my mom, who worked full-time too. Every night he came home from his day job and wrote for thirty minutes before he made our dinner, et cetera. It took him many years to complete the dissertation, but the day finally came when it was done. One day I was complaining to him about time, and he just said, if you want to, write for thirty minutes a day; it's not a lot, but you can write a book that way. That's one lucky thing about being a poet: you can write a book in small installments, if you are greedy enough to seize them.

DB: Let's go back to the question of culture. You have written about poetry, nineteenth-century novels, the movies (okay, film), issues of gender and work, and more. Poetry seems to me to be thriving, yet is also surrounded by a kind of invisible fence; all the poets are inside the yard, yapping to get out, but are out of reach of everyone else walking by. Could you say something about how you see the art today, both as a poet and as a commentator on the state of contemporary culture?

MO'R: This is an important question—so I'll try to offer a few sketched-out thoughts. It's an interesting cultural dilemma, it seems to me. On the one hand, when an art form loses its wider audience and begins to speak mostly to its practitioners, what gets lost is the impulse to relevance, to speak *to* the public. The rise of the M.F.A. program and the transformation of poetry from a public art to a clubbier one have also corresponded to plenty of aesthetic in-fighting, as one might expect. As an editor at a magazine rather than a professor at an academic institution, I feel fairly distanced from the debates and the gossip, and I still read in an eclectic, less-than-doctrinaire way. Sometimes I fear that this makes me less serious than other poets, who live and breathe contemporary poetry, and at other times I think it's what has enabled me to continue loving poetry—to love it in a private, internal way that has more in common with how I read as a child (out of hunger and curiosity) than with any certainty that I know what is "right" or the "best."

As a cultural commentator, though, I always wonder if the poets really *are* yapping to get out from behind the fence. Yes, I imagine that many poets feel a certain amount of frustration at not being able to make a living selling books of poetry, and a certain amount of frustration—or anxiety—at knowing that our work will reach only a small audience. That's a real frustration. On the other hand, the M.F.A. system, whatever its faults, has created a thriving, self-sufficient economy, one that allows many, many writers to have time to write, and also provides them with an engaged, literate audience. In a way the whole world reminds me of ants in a sugar bowl—have you ever seen that? Once they get in, they industriously build a series of ant hills out of sugar, delighted to be in the bowl and have all that sweetness at their disposal. They can't get back out, and yes, they're separated from the other foods by the walls of the bowl, but why should they complain? They're in a bowl of sugar.

DB: Your ants remind me of Thoreau's ants. For him they're a figure of great industry and selfless contribution. Less delight than devotion and habit, I think. And the work of survival.

MO'R: Yes, absolutely. I don't mean to suggest anything frivolous by my metaphor—ants have a tremendous sense of industry, and I consider the work poets do to be a true contribution to our society. In fact, it seems to me that poetry actually is more necessary and more relevant than ever, given our nation's political and social woes, and our age's distractibility. For one thing, the Internet is a wonderful platform for making poetry more accessible to curious readers—and it's also the one medium that can fluidly unify the spoken and the written tradition.

DB: That's the open secret of *Slate,* isn't it? As an Internet magazine, it presents work that is both immediately and hugely accessible; and more so, it is all open to active reply. You invite a forum of response. News and opinion as engagement rather than as mere reception. Do you see a similar kind of development or future for online poetry? Do you see any perils there?

MO'R: I've been wondering about this recently. Is there any way to make a home for poems online that is different from their home in a book? I don't think we know yet. I mean, is there a way to write poetry that draws on the visual and the aural, that uses the flexibility of the medium—poems designed *for* the Internet rather than simply poems reproduced *on* the Internet? The peril of such a question is that it belittles, in some way, the purity of the form itself. Black print on a white page has served literature well for a long time. But I do believe poets should be open—and curious—about how the Internet might change things, offering a folk culture of its own.

DB: Do you find, do you regularly read, Internet literature or poetry sites? I'm thinking about your reply—to find uses for the flexibility of the medium, as you say. Would you suggest any such poets or sites for our audience here?

MO'R: I do look at a site like *Poetry Daily* pretty regularly, and I like that site as an aggregator of good poems. There is that online journal *Blackbird.* But otherwise, no, other than blogs that touch on poetry (which I do look at sometimes).

DB: You have recently added to your *Slate* duties, as we've noted, by becoming co-poetry editor of the *Paris Review.* You have made a fundamental change from Richard Howard's practice of publishing lots of poets. You are doing portfolios now—several pages of poems—by only two or three poets in each issue. Can you say why that's appealing to you?

MO'R: The idea came from the *Paris Review*'s editor, Philip Gourevitch, but both Charlie and I found it appealing. Poetry is intimidating for many readers. We thought that the *Paris Review* might usefully be a place where readers got to linger a little more in a poet's world, to immerse him or herself in the motifs and tropes and music and gestures of that author—whether it's an old pro like John Ashbery or a young poet, like Emily Moore, an emerging writer whose work we recently published. The hope was that after reading five or six poems the reader would come away with the sense of having been firmly introduced to a voice—a full conversation, if you will. The downside is obvious: We miss out on great "one-off" poems, and we get to publish fewer poets. That's a disadvantage both Charlie and I take seriously. As a result, we're now publishing groups of single or double poems in every other issue. I hope that this offers the best of both worlds.

DB: I really like that latest idea, single or double poems in alternating issues with the portfolios. The portfolio does permit real attention and the possibility of seeing one poet's range, but it's nice to see several poets, too. I know, either way, you must read zillions of new poems now. Sometimes it feels to me as though there are so many new poems that I can hardly see through them—so many poems of every kind and subject, it's even hard to see trends. But I'd be awfully interested to hear what you may observe as tendencies or trajectories in the newest poetry. What's going on that interests you mostly deeply, or what holds the greatest promises? Likewise, would you name two or three emerging poets you are excited about, and tell why their work is distinctive?

MO'R: I can't see the forest for the trees, I'm afraid. Generally while reading submissions I am less interested in trying to spot a trend than in simply finding a poet whose voice seems distinctive. I do notice a few things happening broadly: the fruitful use of scientific language and tropes—for example, there is a young woman named Jessica Johnson, a science graduate student, I believe, who has written some poems about jellyfish and the moon—imagining the moon as a kind of snail—that we are publishing. I have been impressed with a book I just read by Peter Streckfus, a young poet who recently won the Yale Younger Series Prize. He has a very strange mind, and it strikes me as an original one—his poems appear to have Asian and Buddhist influences, but they're far more otherworldly than other Asian-influenced poets I know. What is most striking, to tell the truth, is the relative absence of oppositional camps; we don't live in an age of debate about what Lowell called "the raw and the cooked"; instead, the work I see ranges pretty broadly from the personal to sociohistorical.

DB: Now that your own book is about to enter the world, I wonder if you have more to say about the reception of poetry. I mean, especially, those first critical book reviews. You review poetry sometimes yourself. That seems an honorable and imperiled art. What's the job of a poetry reviewer?

MO'R: It is an honorable and imperiled art, and I wouldn't call myself one of its true practitioners. There are people who regularly review poetry, whereas I am more like an enthusiast. I mostly write about poets whose work I can be positive about, and I tend to turn down assignments that involve reviewing a poet whose work I don't like very much. I try to write pieces that explain the gestures and impulses of a given poet and place them in a broader social-historical context, but my hope is that those pieces could be understood by a smart, curious person who doesn't necessarily read lots of poetry. The model I try to emulate is of the critic as explainer; I'm less interested in trying to promote a kind of poetry than in laying bare the mechanics of a style, so that readers, knowing a little more about what, say, a John Ashbery poem is up to, can draw their own conclusions.

It's an odd moment for poetry reviewing. Writing about poetry in outlets like the *New Yorker* or the *New York Times*—or *Slate*—is really different today than it was thirty years ago, because the audience has become ever more balkanized, ever more divided between aficionados and readers who don't know very much about poetry. Figuring out how to write reviews that appeal to both constituencies has been challenging for our literary institutions themselves, it seems to me. I think that's why we've seen an up-tick in snarky reviews that poke fun at the world of poetry as much as they tackle issues in the work. Witty viciousness is effective, and we need reviews that aren't anodyne, but this is only one approach among many.

DB: Yes, I guess witty viciousness is effective, given the vanilla flavoring of so many reviews. But we have a few notable critics for whom viciousness becomes a kind of violence or who are so charmed by their own bile that their reviews are more about them than the work. You know what I mean? Or those critics whose aesthetic seems geared precisely and only to their own poetry.

How does a critic find the right balance of useful and critical rigor without either pandering or extreme brutality? Which reviewers and critics do you find particularly interesting now?

MO'R: I think you're right that many of our best poetry critics write most (or most favorably) about work that reflects their aesthetic as writers. One problem facing American poetry criticism today is that we have no one making coherent sense of everything happening. Is it possible to do that any more, I wonder? Or do all these different aesthetics out there mean that it is impossible for someone to try to make sense of it all? I wonder.

I do believe, though, that it's not that hard to find a balance between pandering and extreme brutality. It just requires an extreme fidelity to one's own aesthetic perceptions and—less hubristically—a willingness to reveal one's own weaknesses, or impulses, as a reader. Then it's possible to be straightforward and fierce without being mean.

As for younger critics, among those who write for magazines and newspapers, Stephen Burt—a friend—has always struck me as a thoughtful and astute critic. I have my points of disagreement with him, but he's smart and always interesting. I think Adam Kirsch is also astute, though our taste is very different; even when I disagree with a piece, what's clear is that he has a set of aesthetic criteria he takes pains to establish. James

Longenbach is wonderful, I think, and I particularly liked his last book *The Resistance to Poetry*. There are others, including the older guard like Helen Vendler.

DB: We've talked about the specialization of poetry and also about the wider reach of Internet audiences. Most of the readers of the *Kenyon Review* are not poetry specialists, though they are widely literate and full of curiosity. To those readers—may their numbers flourish and increase—what can lyric poetry bring to them? I guess another way of asking this is: why read lyric poetry?

MO'R: Well, why not? A lyric poem delivers its payload efficiently. It doesn't require an extraordinary investment of time on the reader's part. So you can figure out quickly whether you like something. More important, the lyric poem is the most powerful embodiment of the paradoxes of life and art. Walter Pater once talked about "the splendour of our experience and of its awful brevity," a phrase I like because it contains both the unutterable depth of perception that living seems to contain and the peculiar corollary—that that depth, those perceptions, are unsustainable because we die. Poems have always seemed to me to be the most crystalline reflection of that sensation of privilege and loss. They mimic life, if you will.

DB: That phrase from Pater is incredible. I think it clarifies for me, a little further, some of the power of your particular poems. Splendor and brevity. The poems in front of us speak in compressed or compacted terms of complex experiences—family relationships, the tortures and oddities of cultural history, the grief of all this brevity. You say in "Peep Show," that there's "no time for this." The waves are fading, and the girls are "glancing at the clock." Yet poetry requires of us a deliberate reading, slow and thoughtful. Are there any final things you hope these five poems might extend to our readers?

MO'R: It's a cliché, but that they might extend a renewed sense of wonder, even mystery. That they might be, as Primo Levi once put it, neither servile nor false; and that by being, in their way, skeptical, ironic, and aware, they might restore the capacity for wonder and for seeing freshly the conditions of our age—or, in a phrase I love from John Ashbery, that they might make a reader experience a "recurring wave of arrival." That's what I'd wish for, at least.

Carl
Phillips

CARL PHILLIPS was born in 1959 in Everett, Washington. He received his A.B. in Greek and Latin from Harvard University in 1981 and his M.A.T. in Latin and classical humanities from the University of Massachusetts in 1983, after which he taught Latin in Massachusetts's high schools for eight years. He returned to Harvard as a doctoral student in classical philology but moved to Boston University where he received his M.A. in creative writing in 1993. Since 1993 he has held a joint position in English, creative writing, and African American studies at Washington University in St. Louis. He is also a widely sought teacher and workshop leader, having taught often at the Bread Loaf Writers' Conference and the M.F.A. program for writers at Warren Wilson College, and having held visiting positions at the University of Iowa, Harvard University, Northwestern University, and elsewhere.

Phillips's books of poetry have appeared rapidly since 1992, with the appearance of his Samuel French Morse Award-winning *In the Blood,* followed by *Cortege* (1995), *From the Devotions* (1998), and *Pastoral* (2000), all published by Graywolf Press. His subsequent poetry collections have appeared from Farrar, Straus, & Giroux: *The Tether* (2001), *Rock Harbor* (2002), *The Rest of Love* (2004), *Riding Westward* (2006), *Quiver of Arrows: Selected Poems 1986–2006* (2007), *Speak Low* (2009), and most recently *Double Shadow* (2011). For his books he has been awarded such prestigious honors as the Kingsley Tufts Prize, the Academy of American Poets Fellowship, an Award in Literature from the American Academy of Arts and Letters, induction into the American Academy of Arts and Sciences, and fellowships from the Guggenheim Foundation and the Library of Congress.

In addition to his poetry, Phillips is an influential critic, literary scholar, and translator. His articles—ranging from the poetry of George Herbert to the problematic of the prose poem to the issue of identity in African American poetry—appear regularly in periodicals like *American Poet, Field,* and *New England Review.* In 2003 his translation of Sophocles's *Philoctetes* was published by Oxford University Press, and in 2004 his critical collection, *Coin of the Realm: Essays on the Life and Art of Poetry,* appeared from Graywolf.

Almost Tenderly

It had the heft of old armor—like a breastplate
of bronze; like a shield, on hinges. It swung apart
like a door. Inside it, the sea was visible—the sea
and, on the shore, a man: stripped; beaten. Very
gently—tenderly, almost—as if to the man, to
calm him, but in fact to no one, the sea was singing:
Here, in the deepening blue of our corruption, let

love be at least one corruption we chose together.
But the man said nothing. *Why not call restlessness
our crown, and our dominion,* sang the sea . . . But
the man was a brokenness like any other: moving,
until it fails to move—the way, over time, suffering
makes no difference. His wounds were fresh; still open.
Where the light fell on them, they flashed, like the sea.

Conquest

Speaking to himself, I think, not me, *You have wanted*
more than was yours to wish for, he said—as if even
to wishing the laws of modesty and excess could be applied,
and should be. We slept. I dreamed.
                                        We'd sworn
never to do harm; then sworn instead to keep trying hard
not to—A kind
            of progress . . .

        • •

                        In the dream, he was powerful:
a hawk,
        or hawk-like—this time, easily distinguishable
from the gentler animals and that relentlessness with which,
like beaten slaves by now
                        used to it, they rise, and they fall.

Tell Me a Story

Maybe this is the prettiest time for it, each tree
but a variation on the governing form, here,
a leaflessness more like death than sleep, less like
singing than remembering what it meant, once,
to sing—and the memory, enough. Though it seems
too early, already there are buds on the star-magnolia—
so soft, they feel like a buck's first set of antlers,
just beginning to show . . . When I touch them,

something rises inside me, that I at first mistake
for gratitude, and then for regret. It descends, then
settles, like a flock of waterfowl on water, the particular
beauty that attends oblivion attending them also, in
their back-and-forthing, and even after that, when,
as I understand it, they'll have grown very still.

Next Stop, Arcadia

There's a man asking to be worshipped only.
He looks inconsolable; rugged; like those
once-popular, but hardly seen anymore,
portraits—depictions, really—of Jesus.
There's another man. He wants to be
flogged while naked and on all fours—
begging for it; no mercy; he says *Make me
beg.*
          There's a field nearby. Stretch of field—
like the one they say divides prayer from
absolute defeat. Here's where the pack-horse,
scaring at nothing visible, broke its tether;
no sign of it since. You know this field:
a constant stirring inside an otherwise great
stillness that never stops surrounding it,
the way memory doesn't, though memory
is not just a stillness,
                                but a field that stirs.
The two men—they've gone nowhere.
They've got questions. Like *Which one's
the field you can actually remember?* and
*Which one's the one you're only imagining
now—standing inside it, staying there,
stay,*
          until it looks like home? Who are they
to be asking questions? You look from one man
to the other. You keep looking—but between
submission, or the seeming resistance that,
more often than not, lately, comes just
before it,
                    which is better? It's hard to decide:
the ugliness of weeping, or the tears themselves?

The Life You Save

After the pinefields, there's the marsh—you can
see it
       from here. *And after that?* History
ending; myth, as it starts
              to stir. *And after that?*

    • •

After that, just the turning back again. Nothing you
won't know already:
            the pinefield; the marsh—
And the reeds, too? The reeds that grow there?

    • •

Yes,
     and the reeds that grow there: beautiful;
invasive; they jostle
         in the smallest wind.
Soon it will be as if nothing had ever happened.

Wrestling toward a Temporary Answer

A Conversation with Carl Phillips

David Baker: Carl, thanks so much for the chance to talk about your five new poems. These are wonderful poems, and we are especially pleased for the chance to print them in our new anniversary issue. We're marking the seventieth year of publication for our magazine. I hope we also have time and the chance during this back-and-forth discussion to talk about your latest projects—poetry and prose—as well as your poetic background and your sense of the coming directions or opportunities for American poets.

I have some questions I'd like to ask about specific poems in this grouping. But I'd like to take the chance to see if you wish to say anything about these poems first—origins, challenges, questions, or whatever you might wish to say to begin.

Carl Phillips: About the poems themselves, well, I suppose they come from my usual resistance to accepting that there are some questions that can't be finally, absolutely answered. These poems were mostly written last fall and early this spring, a period when I seem to have gotten interested especially in power, the ways in which sexual power and political power are analogous, the uneven distribution of power, the costs of that. . . . I can't say I was conscious of any of that while writing the poems, and it's only now, for this interview, that I've stepped back to see what the poems might have in common. Of course, I look at "Tell Me a Story," and that seems to have nothing to do with power—but I suppose oblivion is one form of respite from being consciously bound to power structures.

DB: The issue of power is fascinating. In these poems I follow the rigor and decay of sexual power. It's a familiar trope in your work. The two lovers trade identities of stronger and weaker, or aggressor and submitter, back and forth, and much of the language (of conquest, vanquishment, injury, peacefulness, surrender) reinforces this relationship. I am less clear about the political issue, though of course gender and sexuality can be read as politically textual.

So do you mean that you see your poems, about the dynamics of sexual power, as analogues to a larger political circumstance? Sex as imperialism? Two lovers' relationship as a country of their own, a dominion of two?

CP: Yes. Exactly. In a poem from *The Tether,* I made an attempt to be more overt about that—a poem called "Roman Glass," that speaks of the erosion of the Republic and the rise of Empire in ancient Rome, an analogue, I believe, for the diminishment of shared power in a relationship, and the total assumption of power on the part of an individual.

DB: "Roman Glass" is an important poem in *The Tether.* As you say, it's a poem that articulates the connection between the large political dynamic and the lovers' miniature world. You set about the task, as you say, of "recognizing the folly of equal rule" in that poem.

But let me push on the trope. You seem to find an insistent or at least recurring use of the metaphor of ruling, of sovereignty and servitude, when describing the lovers' relationship, not just in this poem but in the overall scheme of your poetry. Does one lover "rule" the other? Must one? I'm wondering if the trope is exclusive or total, or more like an enabling conceit for your poetry.

CP: I think the obsession with sovereignty and servitude has a lot to do with another obsession, sadomasochism, and the ways in which it can be viewable politically, spiritually, and in terms of the role of trust when it comes to intimacy. As I understand it, in S and M, there are fairly fixed roles. That's interesting—to me—to think about in the context of a relationship between lovers. I used to believe in something like fixed roles, but over the years I very much believe that it's necessary for there to be, if not an occasional exchange of power, then at least an ongoing willingness to renegotiate the terms of power. How that works in the poems, I don't know, but it's how I have lived my life off the page.

DB: That would be what you mean by "folly" then, right? The notion of equality—a democratic rather than colonial or monarchic structure—is a fiction, a folly. So, in your work, the position and use of power transfers back and forth, rather than remains in static equilibrium.

I want to come back to this issue of imbalance, shortly, to talk about some elements of your style. But for now let's turn back to the present group of *Kenyon* poems.

We are really pleased to offer our readers these particular five new poems of yours. Do they come from a new large project? A manuscript of poems? If so, can you say anything about it?

CP: "Conquest" is from my new book, *Speak Low,* which will come out next spring. I find it hard to sum up what that book is about—I suppose something to do with crossing that point beyond which there's no return, the ways in which we fail one another almost willfully, or so it seems, the price of freedom, the intoxicating nature of desire. That last one, of course, isn't all that new a theme for me, but I realize more and more that I'm one of those poets who pushes more deeply at something with each book, as opposed, perhaps, to casting the net more widely, in terms of subject matter. It's why I think of all of my books as a single sustained kind of meditation on—oh, on the ways in which the forces of being human (desire, for example, loss, conquest) shape a sensibility over time. . . . Hmm, I have strayed from the question. Anyway, the other four poems are just poems I've written. I never know what the next manuscript will be or particularly concern. I wait until I feel I have enough poems for a manuscript, and start to think about how they might be working together.

DB: I have a few more questions to ask about individual poems among these five, but I'd like to talk about them all together for a bit longer. They represent new directions for you and they also carry forward some of your more familiar thematic, narrative, and imagistic characteristics.

Do I detect the presence of the sonnet? I can't recall more than a very small handful of sonnets from your previous eight books, and now four of these are sonnets or derivations of sonnets?

CP: Yes, I do think of these as bearing some relationship to the sonnet, though I can't say I had that intention initially. When "Conquest" turned out to be fourteen lines after I'd arranged the lines, I was interested in the degree to which I could call it a sonnet. But after that, I began writing poems that kept coming in around twelve to sixteen lines, and I did start to work more deliberately at getting them to sonnet length. I don't know why this sort of thing happens. In *Riding Westward,* I had become very fond of long lines and blockier-looking stanzas. It's as if this is the natural next response to that.

DB: "Tell Me a Story" and "Almost Tenderly" are the two poems here that most apparently derive from the sonnet. I mean by this not just the eight-and-six structure of "Tell Me a Story" and the seven-seven structure of "Almost Tenderly"; but also I mean to identify places where the voltas fall, where the poems turn, where and how they open, and where, in the final couple of lines, they recapture or recapitulate each narrative.

"The Life You Save" and "Conquest" seem less like traditional sonnets and more akin to, say, a Charles Wright-like rendition. For example, where the dropped and indented partial lines do count toward the fourteen lines of the whole form. "Conquest" even breaks in half with an asterisk at the turn, while "The Life You Save" exploits the three-part Shakespearean form.

CP: Yes, I had hoped that that would be the effect. I get pretty impatient with people who consider any fourteen-line poem to be a sonnet. The turns of thought are crucial, as is the number of turns.

DB: Do you have more sonnets? Why the sonnet and why now?

CP: I think I have one more, written pretty recently. And a couple of short poems, but they're not sonnets. I think it's just something I stumbled into, though. A more recent poem is around eighty lines long, so that's definitely not sonnet territory.

DB: Then let me turn to another issue among these poems. "Almost Tenderly" is a good representation of your work, it seems to me, with its combination of lucidity and mystery. The landscape with its touch of the middle ages and of myth-making is vivid, full of details. The narrative of the broken man is visceral in its portrayal. And the overall examination of "suffering" is something I find in many of your strongest poems.

But just as vivid here is the mysterious primary pronoun "it." This little word may be easy to overlook, but it seems central to fully understanding the poem.

What is "it"? Something grand, like myth? Or something tangible, like a real artifact? Inside "it", we find the whole narrative. Does it matter whether or not we can identify "it"?

CP: I can honestly say I have no idea what the "it" is supposed to refer to. Maybe a certain emotional or psychological state that can't be articulated except in terms of what it could be imagined to contain, if it could be made more concrete. I liked the idea of a poem working like this, an idea I first saw in a poem by Jack Gilbert, "Registration," where a man looks into the worm-opened chest of an owl and sees the city of Byzantium. The rest of the poem is a description of what's going on in Byzantium, and the owl gets completely forgotten—just the means by which the rest of the poem comes into being.

DB: A second familiar characteristic of this poem is also something not immediately assertive. But all five poems bear this touch. I mean the quality of metaphor, especially the rich and abundant similes. Again in "Almost Tenderly" the whole poem and its narrative come to us as simile; the whole poem answers the question of what "it" is "like." As the poem proceeds, one simile transforms into another, and another; the scheme of the whole poem is to open up this tactic, as though inside a single gesture we might find a miniature world, perhaps like the Gilbert poem. Even inside the figurative "wounds" we find a whole sea.

CP: I guess that's to do with how I see the world in general, ramification after ramification, everything sort of divigatory, which probably explains my looping sentences at times. It's a difficult way of thinking, let me tell you. A little maddening.

DB: I think I'll come back to those looping sentences in a bit. How conscious are you, as you write, of the larger governing tactics of your poems like the one we're talking about? And what more might you say about the importance of metaphor—especially simile—to your work? I invite readers to look back over these five poems and find the similes; they are everywhere and they provide the essential magic of the poems. That great "as if."

CP: I'm not conscious of tactics like this at all when I'm writing. It's often the kind of thing I don't notice until I get to the stage of trying to assemble poems into a manuscript. I'll suddenly realize how often certain words appear, but also how often certain strategies come into the poems. It's often how I figure out which poems to eliminate, if too many are working in the same way. As for metaphor and simile, I seem to be very much caught up in abstraction in my work, and I think the only way to deal with abstraction in ways that can bring it more physically into the light is through figuration. Otherwise, a poem would risk sounding ponderous, academic—figuration makes it all more visceral, I find.

DB: I know what you mean. In your poems the abstract is contextualized through figures, tropes. The abstract is made tangible, almost bodily.

There's another trope, an aspect of landscape, which recurs not just in these poems but back through several books of yours. I mean, the field, the pastoral expanse. It's a landscape of birds, waves, ponds and marshes, pine fields, horses. Sometimes it seems lifted from medieval settings, or classical ones, and sometimes it is contemporary. As you say yourself in "Falling" (one of my favorite poems in *Riding Westward*), "There's a meadow I can't stop coming back to." You go so far as to identify this place as your "sacred grove." I am tempted to think this is a view from your window on Cape Cod. So tell me, what field do you see? And is it invested with holiness because of its profound presence in your imagination? Or is there a different explanation for its holiness?

CP: On the Cape, the view from my window is all forest—many acres of conservation land. I really became keen on fields when I moved to the Midwest, and started going out into the landscape with my partner Doug, who was always looking for good photos at sunset. Fields became something I could love in the way that I love the ocean when I'm out east.

About holiness, I don't know that I can think of holiness as anything more than how we choose to invest a space with—variously—belief, the will to believe, the refusal to have a thing be "merely" what it is. . . . I know that's a little vague.

DB: Then let me ask a related, maybe larger question about this subject. What is the connection for you between the world—with its multitudes, its failures and damages and beauties, all of its secular and natural particularities—and the sacred?

CP: Well, again, I'm uneasy about concepts of the sacred and of holiness. If I believe in the sacred at all, it's more in the sense of finding something to have a sacred sort of resonance for me—maybe this is something like the sublime? In the sudden scattering of leaves from a tree, I feel something sacred, but I don't think the moment itself has sacred value, that it's a sign—I'm not a transcendentalist or anything. . . . I want to believe that things mean more than they do. But I have my doubts. But I want to believe that my doubts might also mean more than they do.

DB: Yes, this does sound like the sublime—the awareness of beauty so immense or amorphous that we fear for our safety or sanity. And it is related to the transcendental, especially if that term can suggest something other than the conventionally religious. Maybe instead of the religious, we are talking about the ineffable or the numinous—the thing suggested beyond the thing in front of us.

You say you feel uncomfortable with these concepts. But they are—like the trope of the politicized lovers that we discussed earlier—a central part of your poetic, your language, even your method of figuration. I think I mean your amazing capability to suggest that-which-is-beyond presence or the present moment. Maybe again we're talking about the deepest operation of metaphor, the exchange of thing for thing, or the association of thing for thing. Would that be in the ballpark?

CP: I hope I won't sound like I'm being difficult, if I say that these things are not tropes, for me, they're just how I think and what I think. I guess they become tropes, for readers, once the poem exists, but for me there's not very much separation between the poem and the life behind it.

DB: So do you think metaphor itself is a kind of holiness? Or is that going too far? I know some of your favorite forebears—Herbert and Donne, Dickinson and Hopkins—would likely make that association between metaphor and the sacred.

CP: I don't think metaphor itself is a kind of holiness—but I believe that the ability to see in terms of metaphor is a special kind of vision. In that sense, I lean towards the ancient Greco-Roman idea of the vatic, the way in which access to certain kinds of vision can be viewed as a kind of holiness.

DB: Can you say more about that? What kinds of vision? And how does one gain access?

CP: The kind of vision I mean is the kind that makes some people poets and others not. Or maybe I should say, it makes some poets the poets they are—I'm not speaking here of the kind of poetry that seems merely a record of the world as anyone on the street would be likely to see it. I mean the kind that presents the world as if for the first time. As to how that kind of vision is accessed—I suspect there's no method. Strategy can be taught, when it comes to poetry, but not vision.

DB: Some of your favorite poets seem to me to pick up and continue this idea of the Greco-Roman vatic. I'm thinking, as I said just above, of Herbert and Donne, Dickinson, Hopkins, maybe Geoffrey Hill. I see in these poets, and in your own work, a shared style, too, in addition to the vatic or prophetic. These poets are metaphysical—dense, very complicated in everything from their treatment of image and conceit to syntax and phrasing.

Is that accurate to say? And if so, then does the vatic seem metaphysical to you?

CP: I guess it can be, but I don't think that's the only possible manifestation of the vatic.

DB: You've touched on a few more stylistic issues but we haven't addressed them fully yet. You mentioned your looping sentences, and your recent application, sometimes, of a blockier form on the page.

Your syntax is characterized not only by long constructions, but also, within those long constructions, by all manner of interruptions. You are parenthetical, self-interrupting, hesitant, delaying, and all of those tactics seem to me to achieve an amazing result. In your best work, the sentence itself creates something like an analogue for thinking. I feel an idea being glimpsed, doubted, tried out, explained, absorbed, rejected, by turns. Most poets aspire to a sentence that seems the result of thinking; yours mimic the very processes of perception and cognition as they happen.

CP: Maybe this gets back to what I said about the lack of separation between life and poem that comes from a life. I think most poets are overly self-conscious of being poets; they are very much aware that they are trying to articulate something on a page, and they often seem to be very much aware of an audience outside themselves. I'm not at all like that. I work intuitively, wrestling toward a temporary answer to questions that emerge from a struggle that is ultimately utterly private. I think I'm just lucky that my private struggles happen to be, as well, human struggles, so that the poems happen to resonate with other people besides myself. But I've never expected that, or sought it. It's why I can easily swing into anxiety when I'm giving a reading—it truly feels like I'm revealing something very private. Of course, it's not as if the poems are baldly confessional, and the actual struggle, the specifics of it, are never in the poem; that's part of the transformative work that a poem has to do. But I myself know what the source of a given poem was, and it can be wrenching to bring that up again, and in public.

DB: Your poems do shimmer with a sense of intimate revelation, sheer exposure. I never read your poems as bluntly autobiographical, though—but rather as gestures toward connection with the reader. The paradox of this connection is that it comes out of highly private-sounding narratives. But Whitman showed us this paradox, didn't he? The "dark patches" of "Crossing Brooklyn Ferry" served as his bleakest confessions but also as his means of physical connection.

So how do you maneuver from the baldly personal, as you say, to the artistic? Is that how conceit and myth work, to aid in that transformation?

CP: I really think it's been luck, in my case, since I work pretty intuitively and from a deeply private space. How the work produced there ends up having a wider resonance remains a mystery to me, and I have to admit, I think it's best that it remain a mystery. I think it's true that myth, in particular, can be a way to transform the personal into something less so, but it's not a guarantee.

DB: Privacy and intimacy. The poems in your later work—I'm thinking of *Pastoral* and since then—have often explored the intimate life of a gay man. You have pursued a gay narrative with increasing openness and depth.

We are all of us made of many selves. You refer to this phenomenon as the "many-sidedness of self" in your essay "Boon and Burden: Identity in Contemporary American Poetry." Another side of your own self is an African American man. How do issues of racial identity affect your poems? I think you think of yourself at times as a gay poet. How do you think of yourself as a black poet?

CP: Well, for the record, I don't think of myself as having pursued a gay narrative specifically, but a narrative of what it means to be human—the issues I'm interested in aren't limited to gay men, any more than they are limited to African Americans. I see myself as a poet who happens to be black and gay, just as he happens to be from Massachusetts, just as he happens to live in Missouri. All of these are powerful lenses through which I see the world. It's true that being black and gay gets particular responses in the world—one is more likely to have felt rejected for being gay than for being from Missouri, for example. But I don't go around consciously thinking of myself as anything in particular, when it comes to identity. Or I believe that identity is so much more than race and sexual orientation.

DB: Again in "Boon and Burden" you say you want "neither to compromise [your] individuality nor to be restricted by the particulars of it." Do you mean then, in your poetry, that these facets of a self—sexual preference, for instance, or gender or racial identity—are aspects to be transcended, or to be embraced, or both?

CP: I want them to become more broadly resonant—not irrelevant, exactly, yet not the point.

DB: I'd like to turn now more deeply to issues of style. Let's look at one of the *Kenyon* poems. This is the looping kind of construction we've been talking about. In "Conquest" the first four lines typify that style. The very long first sentence begins with a participle phrase, then asserts a quick self-revealing interruption ("I think"), then the italic addition of another voice, then a dash followed by a qualifying clause, itself capable of commenting on itself ("and should"). Then the punch of those two tiny sentences that follow. It's wonderful pacing.

CP: Those two tiny sentences were the hardest to write, believe it or not. The longer sentence is simply my mind doing its wandering thing again.

DB: So now I really like the adjustment from the sturdy first stanza into the falling-apart of the second: the uneven lines, the interruptions ("instead" and the dash), and finally the fading of the ellipses. And this all recollects, and starts again, in the final stanza with the assurance of the new narrative, the new trope of the dream. It seems to me a large task accomplished in a very compressed space.

We can find more of those very long sentences (with their hesitations, inclusions, self-references, quick veers-away) in all five of these poems. Do you have a model in mind when you write this way?

CP: I don't have a model in mind, no. I really do think this way. But it's also true that my thinking may well have been shaped by my interest in inflected language, and in particular in the Latin of Tacitus and Cicero, both of whom can effectively mix the long sentence with an unexpected moment of terseness, the terseness gaining all the more power because of its appearance in the context of lengthier sentences. Much later, I discovered Randall Jarrell's "90 North," which culminates in a sentence that is stretched across two or three stanzas, followed with a simple sentence: "It is pain." I get chills every time I read that poem, and I believe it has everything to do with the manipulation of sentence length.

DB: We're back to the issue of imbalance, aren't we? The tension—sexual as well as syntactical—between different elements and degrees of power, and the exchange back and forth of that power.

So let's look at a further stylistic touch—something that accompanies your looping sentences. You often enhance the hesitating sentence—as I'll call that manner of interruption and heavily punctuated movement—by means of your lineation. The long sentence seems longer, and the interrupted sentence seems even more hesitant or deferential, when you shape them into short lines. The line is, of course, yet another manner of punctuation and deliberation. Nothing in a poem is more obvious than the line. This is a structure you have used all along in your work, the long sentence set against the short line.

But I have also been really compelled in your latest work by a few strong poems that have eschewed the short line in behalf of an extended and more regular line. I'm thinking in *Riding Westward* of "Bright World," "Ocean," and maybe the title poem; those are three of my favorite poems in the book. I'm also thinking, even earlier in *The Rest of Love,* of a few poems that seem now to me to be working toward that extended and smoothed-out linear form, poems like "Custom" and "Here, on Earth."

We might look here at "Tell Me a Story" and "Almost Tenderly" as short versions of that effect. Or "Next Stop, Arcadia." What differences are you finding in those methods of lineation? I mean, long regular lines versus short or more various linear constructions.

CP: "Custom" was a breakthrough poem for me, both in terms of its being a single stanza, and in terms of the wildly veering line length. That poem was written last of all the poems in *The Rest of Love,* I believe, so its effects don't get seen until the book after that, *Riding Westward.* Being able to allow a ragged edge to the poem felt very freeing. I'd been so caught up in stanzas that looked neat on the page, and very caught up in lots of pauses, which meant very short lines, with a pause at the end of each of them. At a certain point, I guess this just felt overly dramatic, I don't know. It wasn't a conscious shift—I tried hard to lineate "Custom" differently, and eventually I realized it had already found its form. That's how it always works for me. I'll think I've remained pretty much the same across the various books, and then realize I have been evolving, in my own way, from book to book, outgrowing something or getting bored with it.

The long lines just sound right, when I read the poems aloud—if there is hesitation within sentences, there's an increased confidence in terms of a longer period of time that isn't punctuated with the pause of the line break. And yet, I want a little of both, I suppose, which is where the dropped lines come in, allowing the reader to see the entire line across the page, but also having some of the pause—the psychological caesura—that a dropped line, for me, indicates, a pause, but not as big a pause as an actual line break at the end of a line would indicate.

DB: We've talked about lots of great past poets. But what about today's poets? Who are you reading with interest? What interests you in those poets' work?

CP: I have been looking at poets who write a very short poem, and who push at lineation. Christine Garren, Jean Valentine, recent Frank Bidart, Lyn Hejinian's *The Fatalist,* Martha Ronk. I keep studying and studying the shorter poems in Robert Hass's *Time and Material* . . . I'm back to memorizing sonnets of Shakespeare—whoops, he's not exactly contemporary . . .

DB: What are you seeking in the very short poems you are reading? What are you finding?

CP: I'm trying to see how different writers get so much resonance out of so few words—the power of economy, something that I've always cared about, but I would like to see what would happen if I really started thinking in terms of spareness. The poets I have loved from very early on are Li Po and Tu Fu—that's what first got me thinking about how short a poem can be, and still be a poem. I don't think, in the course of my reading, that I'm finding out the "secret," exactly, since that's different for each poet. But I have usually found that I learn and grow as a writer simply by reading as much as I can, and relying on some sort of osmosis that isn't trackable, but is very real.

DB: And who are your students reading, and why?

CP: It's hard to say what they're reading of their own volition. What I have directed them to in the past semester includes Jarrell, the Hass book mentioned earlier, selections from Bogan, Frost's "Directive." I try to

assign, half the time, reading that they might not have looked into, yet—
this usually means the dead, I have found. The very dead. Or people over
the age of fifty or so—who aren't dead, of course, but for some reason the
younger poets I encounter seem less interested in older generations.
That's a whole other subject. The rest of the time, we look at work by
people who will be visiting the campus—this semester, we'll read Carolyn
Forche, Kay Ryan, and Henri Cole—and work that is sometimes very very
new, a poem I'll have encountered in a recent journal, for example.
Anything that I feel they could learn something useful from.

DB: What do they need to know? I ask that question as a fellow teacher
who has noticed how professional our students have become, especially
those in M.F.A. programs and the bigger summer writing workshops.
They act as though they are going into business, assembling resumes, net-
working, comparing experiences in this or that workshop. What don't
they know that you feel urgent about teaching them?

CP: They need to know that emotion is real, and not only worth spending
time with, but essential to spend time with, if they want their poems to in
any way reflect what it is to have been alive in our time. No matter how
much technology there may be in the world, we are still people, vulnerable
in many ways, and we still turn to poetry as a way of understanding that.

I also think it's important for them to remember that we can only
write the way we write—in terms of style, pace, and sensibility. I often
have students who are anxious to get the first book out there, simply to
get a job, and yet they know they haven't written the book they hope to
write. I understand the pressure, but I think it's really important to try to
ignore it, for the sake of the work. Or I've had students who lament how
they write—they wish they wrote prose poems, or lush nature poems, or
whatever—but they must write the poem they must write. There's no
choice in the matter, it seems to me, without things beginning to sound
forced and inauthentic.

DB: You teach widely. You are a sought-out teacher. How do you feel
about the graduate writing programs and the summer workshops, the
proliferation of them? What value and what peril?

CP: The peril ties in with your last question. Some programs—well,
maybe all of them, to some extent—have a way of making students aware
of a profession beyond the writing program walls, a profession that's com-
petitive and can generate anxieties that are counterproductive to getting
good work done. Programs, by their very nature, suggest that there are
time constraints on production, as does the tenure process—and yet,

great art can't be produced in that way. Finally, I think workshop inevitably makes writers very self-conscious of what they're doing. Sometimes, it's good just to go with something, rather than analyzing why you're doing something a particular way, or agonizing over who did and didn't "get" your poem in workshop.

But the value, for the student who truly comes to a workshop in order to become a better writer, is that a trusted community of writers can allow a writer to look at his or her work through other eyes, and perhaps see the failures and successes that the poet him or herself couldn't quite see. There's also the wonderful exposure to a variety of voices, and this can work the way reading can, to inform one's own work in ways that are very real and intangible.

DB: As you look forward now, to your own new and next work, what do you see? What projects or what questions seem to be emerging for you? That is, how do you see your work growing or changing?

CP: My work tends to change mainly in terms of form—all these sonnet-y pieces suggest that I'm headed that way, at the moment, for reasons unknown. And the questions are the same ones for me, as ever. Who am I? How can I grapple with what I am and wish I wasn't? What am I here for? What is morality? If the questions don't change that much, I hope that my responses do, if only by virtue of my being older and each time coming to the questions with a whole new set of experiences behind me.

DB: Along this same vein, what kinds of things do you think our new and next poets will need to address? This could be formal, this could be thematic —I don't know, but I'm curious about your sense of the forthcoming.

CP: Ah, I have no sense of the forthcoming—and rather like it that way. I think the new poets will inevitably need to address what it means to be alive in our time, in the context of you-name-it: politics, war, catastrophe. In all of those contexts, we still love, and we still sorrow. We remain human beings.

Stanley
Plumly

STANLEY PLUMLY was born in 1939 in Barnesville, Ohio, and grew up in the rural Quaker countryside of Ohio and in western Virginia. He received his B.A. from Wilmington College and his M.A. and Ph.D. from Ohio University. For more than forty years, Plumly has taught in universities around the country—including the universities of Iowa, Houston, Washington, Columbia, and Princeton—and currently holds the Distinguished University Professorship at the University of Maryland, where he has taught since 1985.

Plumly's poetry is notable for the lyricism of its language and for its elegant precision of syntax and story. Rich in details of the natural world and powerful in its human passions, his work has won, in 2002, an award from the American Academy of Arts and Letters as well as many other honors and fellowships. His poetry and prose have appeared in virtually every important literary journal in America, including the *American Poetry Review*, the *Atlantic Monthly*, the *New Yorker*, *Poetry*, and the *Yale Review*.

Stanley Plumly's first book of poems, *In the Outer Dark,* was published in 1970 by Louisiana State University Press. The more recent of his ten books of poetry include *Now That My Father Lies Down Beside Me: New and Selected Poems* (Ecco, 2001), *Old Heart* (W. W. Norton, 2007), and *Orphan Hours* (W. W. Norton, 2012). In 2008 Norton published the culmination of Plumly's two decades of research and writing about the life and poetry of John Keats; *Posthumous Keats: A Meditation on Immortality,* received both wide critical acclaim and popular readership. The third chapter of *Posthumous Keats* appears as "This Mortal Body" in the *Kenyon Review.*

Posthumous Keats

The road is so rough Severn is walking,
and every once in a while, since the season is
beautiful and there are flowers on both sides,
as if this path had just been plowed,
he picks by the handful what he can

and still keep up. Keats is in the carriage
swallowing blood and the best of the bad food.
It is early November, like summer,
honey and wheat in the last of the
daylight, and above the mountains a clear

carnelian heart line. Rome is a week
away. And Severn has started to fill
the carriage with wildflowers—rust, magenta,
marigold, and the china white of cups.
Keats is floating, his whole face luminous.

The biographer sees no glory in this,
how the living, in increments, are dead,
how they celebrate their passing half in love.
Keats, like his young companion, is alone,
among color and a long memory.

In his head he is writing a letter
about failure and money and the ten-
thousand lines that could not save his brother.
But he might as well be back at Gravesend
with the smell of the sea and cold sea rain,

waiting out the weather and the tide—
he might as well be lying in a room,
in Rome, staring at a ceiling stylized
with roses or watching outside right now
a cardinal with two footmen shooting birds.

He can still remember the meadows near
St. Cross, the taste in the air of apples,
the tower and alms-square, and the River
Itchen, all within the walk of a mile.
In the poem it is Sunday, the middle

of September, the light a gold conglomerate
of detail—"in the same way that some pictures
look warm." He has closed his eyes.
And he is going to let the day close down.
He is thinking he must learn Italian.

By the time they reach the Campagna the wind
will be blowing, the kind that begins at sea.
Severn will have climbed back in, finally a
passenger, with one more handful to add
to what is already overwhelming.

Constable's Clouds for Keats

They come in off the sea peaceable masters
and hold the sea in the sky as long as they can.
And you write them down in oils because of their
brilliance, and to remember, in its turn, each one.

It's eighteen twenty-two after the Regency,
and it would be right in the year after his death
to think of these—domed above the Heath
in their isolated chronicle—as elegies

of the spirit; right to see these forms
as melancholy hosts, even at this distance.
Yet dead Keats is amorphous, a shapelessness
re-forming in the ground, and no one you know enough

to remember. He lies in the artist's paradise
in Rome, among the pagan souls of sheep at pasture.
You'll lie in Hampstead where he should have stayed
to meet you on your walks up Lower Terrace

or along the crowning High Street heading home.
Your clouds grow whiter, darker, more abstract
from one elaborate study to the next,
correlatives, or close, to the real sentiment

that lives, you say, in clouds . . . subjects to counter-
weigh the airy gravity of trees and leaping horses.
Keats could have met you—you must have seen him once
against the light, at least. He could be

crossing on Christchurch Hill Road now, then
over to the Elm Row and down Old Admiral's Walk.
He could be looking at the clouds blooming between
buildings, watching the phantoms levitating stone.

He was there your first Heath summer writing odes,
feeling the weather change from warm to chill,
focused, no less than you, on daylight's last detail,
wondering what our feelings are without us.

This Mortal Body (excerpt)

Yet can I gulp a bumper to thy name,—
O smile among the shades, for this is fame!

1.

On June 22, 1818, two years to the day before he sat in Leigh Hunt's living room having his one and only tea with the Gisbornes, John Keats and his brother George and his brother's bride, Georgiana, along with Charles Brown, boarded the Prince Saxe Cobourg Liverpool coach, bound west-northwest through "Stony-Stratford, Lichfield, and the Potteries." It was a Monday morning, and they left just before noon, expecting to arrive in the port of Liverpool thirty-two hours later. They all probably rode on the top of the coach, both for the view and the reduction in expense. In all likelihood, top-heavy, too, was the boot of the coach, since George and Georgiana carried with them their worldly possessions—as much, at least, as could be sensibly borne across the Atlantic to the interior of America. George was dressed like any early eighteenth-century English gentleman —high-collared waistcoat, breeches, stockings, smart shoes; Georgiana, in a high-waisted muslin gown and either a coal-scuttle bonnet or a country straw hat tied under the chin with ribbons. George had just turned twenty-one, Georgiana between seventeen and nineteen, depending on the conjecture of her birth date. Neither one had the bearing, let alone the appearance, of an emigrant. Brown, on the other hand, the inveterate traveler, was flushed out in a tartan suit, a plaid over the shoulder, and a white hat for his bald head, plus an oilskin packed for the rain, a regular "Red Cross Knight," according to Keats. Keats himself, no less noticeable, wore a fur hat, a well-weathered jacket, and a plaid. He and Brown were taking a different kind of journey altogether from the newly married couple—theirs was to be a full-summer walking tour, first of the English Lake District, then north into the Highlands, eventually topping off in John o' Groats, the northernmost point in Scotland, before starting south and home along the North Sea coast.

Tom Keats, in the summer of 1818, was somewhat conspicuous by his absence. The summer before, Tom and George had spent a happy yet expensive time in Paris, while John had lodged in Oxford trying to get his first test at a major poem—Endymion—off the ground. Restlessness was part of all three brothers' dailiness. They were always planning trips, always on the move, whether in town or out of town. Restlessness was one of the results of their orphaning. Fanny Keats, kept like a captive princess within their guardian Abbey's household, must have felt the need to get out and about keenly. By the fall of 1817, however, when the brothers had returned to Hampstead and Well Walk from their various journeys, it was clear that something, perhaps serious, was wrong with Tom. He was already, in fact, spitting blood. Though taller than his older brothers, Tom was also considerably thinner—bird-chested, delicate-featured, more like a Shelley than a Keats. John, the oldest and the shortest, was robust, broad-shouldered, like their father. George was a type in between, medium in height, medium and temperate in every other way. But the bird-like Tom looked frail, always had. It is as if, in the diminuendo of male birth, there had been a falling off in the birthing of the Keats brothers, with John the healthiest, and Edward, the fourth Keats son, dying in childhood. Tom was third in line. Tom's relative health at this moment is crucial because George and John have come of age and in no time so will Tom. Their intimacy with and dependency on one another is beginning to come to closure. George has plans; John has plans; Tom, for some while, seems to have set for himself, involuntarily, a career as a patient.

More travel, in fact, seems to be Tom's only plan. The irony cannot be lost that one of the trips he and John have in mind is that when John returns from his "Scottish tour" they will spend the winter in Italy, with the hopes that a softer climate will make the difference and reverse Tom's "English" illness. In two short years, it will be John, not his brother, as the patient contemplating Italy. For now, though, Tom is resting at their Well Walk address, being attended by friends and Mrs. Bentley, their benevolent landlady. Tom has been, certainly in John's eyes, the sort of heart-center of the triad of the brothers. On one of their most companionable evenings, when they were still living in Cheapside, it is Tom whom Keats celebrates in one of his most tender sonnets, "To My Brothers":

> Small, busy flames play through the fresh-laid coals,
> And their faint cracklings o'er our silence creep
> Like whispers of the household gods that keep
> A gentle empire o'er fraternal souls.
> And while, for rhymes, I search around the poles,

Your eyes are fixed, as in poetic sleep,
Upon the lore so voluble and deep,
That aye at fall of night our care condoles.
This is your birthday Tom, and I rejoice
That thus it passes smoothly, quietly.
Many such eves of gently whispering noise
May we together pass, and calmly try
What are this world's true joys—ere the great voice,
From its fair face, shall bid our spirits fly.

The great voice, fair-faced or otherwise, has been audible within Tom's hearing for longer than either of his brothers has been willing to admit. This poem marks Tom's seventeenth birthday; it also, pretty closely, marks the beginning of the burden his health will represent to George and John, who will for the next year or so alternately serve as companion and nurse. Each of the brothers will suffer the weight and guilt of the experience.

John, in particular, with his medical training and his boyhood nursing of his mother, is well aware of the symptoms of consumption, blood-spitting being the first. This—this late-spring, early-summer period of 1818—is what might be termed, in the young lives of the three Keats brothers, a crossing moment, a moment when certain decisions cannot be reversed, cannot be quite yet understood—"we are in a Mist," writes Keats to John Reynolds in May, from Teignmouth—and cannot be controlled or known for their possible unintended consequences. George, who for so long has brother-sat Tom while John has moved about trying to complete *Endymion*, has decided to strike out on his own: get married and seek opportunity in the New World, especially as, except for companioning his young brother, he has not been gainfully employed for more than a year. ("You know," Keats writes to Benjamin Bailey, "my Brother George has been out of employ for some time. It has weighed very much upon him, and driven him to scheme and turn things over in his Mind.") With the completion of his trial-by-poem, his first attempt at an epic, Keats will now be expected to take over more or less full-time care and concern for Tom. Yet Keats has his own intentions and hopes for the summer, primary among them is "a pedestrian tour through the north of England and Scotland as far as John o' Groats." He has high, ambitious reasons for such a journey, which will "make a sort of Prologue to the Life I intend to pursue—that is to write, to study and to see all Europe at the lowest expence. I will clamber through the Clouds and exist." As for Tom, the last thing he wants to be is a burden, and he, no less than his brothers, closes at least one eye on his true condition, a pattern that will repeat itself when Keats takes on similar symptoms. Just within a few short days in March, for example, Tom's plight goes from "Tom saying how much better he had got" (March 13) to "Poor Tom—who could have imagined such a change" (March 18) to "Tom has been much worse: but is now getting better" (March 21). Throughout the spring and into the summer, the wish for health will obscure the fact of it.

Teignmouth, on the coast of Devon, had been the hoped-for winter retreat from the bone chill of London, with George and John taking turns caring for Tom. Instead it had been storm-wind and horizontal rain almost constantly, which meant—now that John was there in close quarters with his brother, in rooms practically sealed off—an unhealthy proximity, a pattern that would be repeated in the fall, in Hampstead, once John returned from his Northern walks. At fourteen, Keats had already played physician to their mother, whose wasted consumptive body surely rose in his imagination here with the pale, withering Tom, who by this time had begun to hemorrhage. And it takes no imagination to connect Tom to their mother and her several relatives who have died of consumption, and to link that lineage to oneself. Within days of Tom's first violent convulsion of blood, Keats tries to joke away his obvious depression in a telling comment to Bailey, complaining, of all things, about the wet weather. "When a poor devil is drowning, it is said he come thrice to the surface, ere he makes his final sink if however, even at the third rise, he can manage to catch hold of a piece of weed or rock, he stands a fair chance,—as I hope I do now, of being saved." (Hemorrhaging, as Keats will discover, is a lot like drowning.) But as Tom's health, in the weeks ahead, has stabilized, they both feel it is time to return to London, to George, and to the future, a future in which George is soon to join a world of independent responsibilities.

The beginning of the trip from Teignmouth back to London goes well enough—"My Brother has borne his Journey thus far remarkably well," so Keats writes to friends from Honiton. But outside of Bridport, in Dorset, in what will become Hardy-country, Tom has another hemmorhage. Many days later, in a long thank-you note to "Miss Mary Ann Jeffrey / Teignmouth / Devonshire," thanking her for "kind solicitude," Tom writes from Well Walk that "the rest of the journey pass'd off pretty well after we left Bridport in Dorsetshire—I was very ill there and lost much blood—we travell'd a hundred miles in the last two days—I found myself much better at the end of the journey than when I left Tartarey alias Teignmouth—the Doctor was surprised to see me looking so well, as were all my Friends— they insisted that my illness was all mistaken Fancy and on this presumption excited me to laughing and merriment which has deranged me a little—however it appears that confinement and low spirits have been my chief enemies and I promise myself a gradual recovery—."

2.

At the close of the Jeffrey letter, Tom alludes to his much mulled over project of going to Italy—"most likely to the town of Paiva"—where he looks forward to acquiring "a stock of knowledge and strength which will better enable me to bustle through the world—I am persuaded this is the best way of killing time." If John gets back soon enough from his summer "in the Clouds," all the better. They can once again travel together. For the time being, though, "I shall be here alone and I hope well—John will have set out on his Northern Expedition George on his Western . . . John will take four months at the end of that time he expects to have achieved two thousand miles mostly on Foot—George embarks for America." The three brothers, from that June 22 moment when George and John leave Tom very much alone in order to start their separate, disparate journeys, will never be together again. At the port of Liverpool, George, with his bride Georgiana, will sail off into a whole new and unchartable life, far into the rough interior of a new world. John, with his new resolve to put the apprenticeship of Endymion behind him and with his new friend Brown as a tour guide, will test himself in more ways than he can imagine in the next demanding two—not four—months. Tom, of course, will not get to Italy, he will not get anywhere, and will be waiting for John in Well Walk once the abortive Northern tour is over. It may be true of all families of multiple brothers or sisters—of, say, the Brontë sisters, where of the three one dominates and takes on qualities of the other two: becomes, in fact, a resolution of the other two, the way Charlotte, the eldest, combines the lyricism of Emily and the darkness of Anne, the way that Jane Eyre, Wuthering Heights, and The Tenant of Wildfell Hall are aspects of one consciousness—it may be true that siblings of the same sex form a kind of singularity and that one brother or one sister stands out or represents the whole, particularly when they come in threes. George and Tom were not writers, but they were intimates of the work of their elder brother; they were, in their turn, muse and matter in the work.

Until he left for America, George either kept Keats's poems or copied them or both, serving very often as John's agent and social facilitator; indeed, introducing Keats to what became, in history, much of the Keats circle, including Joseph Severn, Charles Dilke, and William Haslam. "George has ever been more than a brother to me, he has been my greatest friend," Keats says in 1818, and a year later, well after George has emigrated, "George always stood between me and any dealings in the world." To the extent that Keats has any practical sense, any job-seeking or money-managing awareness, George represents that grounded part of his character. Tom, on the other hand, "who understood John's character perfectly," and who also, worshipfully, kept copies of his brother's early poems, represents something of the soul of Keats. It is no exaggeration to suggest that Tom's long illness and the long-suffering of their mother's illness and death that it reenacts, along with Tom's and the mother's emotional vulnerability, even innocence, go to the core of Keats. Tom, especially, in so many ways, as a vital yet paling presence, anticipates Keats's maturing, sympathetic contract with the world; he becomes the living correlative for Keats's forgiving emotion. And when Tom does, finally, give in to the consumption that has reduced him to a ghost, just days following his nineteenth birthday—December 1, 1818—he becomes that central quality of imagination we call inspiration, a grief figure that again and again needs to be addressed, reinvoked, reconciled—not simply as a knight-at-arms or a youth grown "pale, and spectre-thin," but as an enlarging emblem, a motivating measure, a rich resource of loss, to which—to paraphrase Wordsworth—the poet repairs as to a fountain. Whatever Tom's literal death meant to Keats—and with George "lost" in the middle of America and Fanny Keats virtually locked away, it meant everything—he becomes for Keats a fountain of an elemental fraternal emotion. "I Have two Brothers one is driven by the 'burden of Society' to America the other, with an exquisite love of our parents and even for early Misfortunes has grown into a affection 'passing the Love of Women'—I have been ill-temper'd with them, I have vex'd them—but the thought of them has always stifled the impression that nay woman might otherwise have made upon me—I have a Sister too and may not follow them, either to America or to the Grave—Life must be undergone, and I certainly derive a consolation from the thought of writing one or two more Poems before it ceases."

These words written a little over a week before George is to set sail certainly imply Keats's state of mind, a melancholy mixture of fatalism, ambition, and profound affection—that "temper that if I were under Water I would scarcely kick to come to the surface"—but they also reveal how necessary family, in one form or another, is to him. George's imminent "disappearance," the thought of it as much as the fact of it, has placed Keats into one of his deepest depressions. Tom's vexing illness and ultimate death will then shift the emotional scale beyond the warp and woof of "despair and energy," as Keats has once characterized it, to something more transforming, since beginning with the winter of 1819 and the escapist "Eve of St. Agnes" through the great spring and autumnal odes of the rest of the evolving year, Keats will discover his full, creative life, the so-called "living year." Tom, in death, will turn into a source, a figure at once ambiguous, exclusionary, and sometimes conspiratorial, a kind of collaborator, whose existential example will both inspire and confirm to Keats that he, too, may die from what has killed his brother. Worse, in the way that news and rumor are passed on, with Tom's death, at the transition between autumn and winter, Keats will sense that he has in fact begun to die; is, in little pieces, dying. "Life must be undergone, and I certainly derive consolation from the thought of writing one or two more Poems before it ceases"—this in a letter to Bailey days before the trip to America and the journey north begin.

Living through It

A Conversation with Stanley Plumly

David Baker: Stan, it's a real pleasure to have this chance to talk about the culmination of your many years of devoted work on the life and poetry of John Keats. People know your poetry, of course, and your critical essays and reviews about contemporary poetry. But fewer are aware that you've been working for a long time on a book about Keats. We are excited for the chance to print "This Mortal Body" in the *Kenyon Review.* I want to start with that essay here, then venture further into the whole project from which this piece is drawn. Then I hope we will have time to discuss your own work, your new poems, and *Old Heart.*

"The Mortal Body" is about the great nineteenth-century British Romantic poet, John Keats. Specifically, you focus in this essay on Keats and his circle in the summer of 1818. Could you place that time in Keats's lifeline for us here just a bit? Why focus on this summer?

Stanley Plumly: The Keats book, as I've come to call it over the years, is titled *Posthumous Keats,* for reasons we can talk about later. The book is in seven chapters, seven sections to a chapter—I couldn't write it any other way than like a poem. The numerology gives it all a certain overt gesture toward structure; that way I can explore, juxtapose, circulate, whatever, within a structure. So that within the "superstructure" of the thing I am permitted asymmetry: none of the sections is equal in length, for instance, and though the chapters function somewhere between forty to forty-five manuscript pages, there is imbalance there, too. The crucial "imbalance"—which brings us to your question about chapter 3—is that at fifty pages this is what I think of as the fulcrum chapter.

DB: Seven chapters, seven sections: that's the structure, seven by seven, of your seminal poem, "Summer Celestial." Maybe we'll come back to that. But would you dive a little more deeply into chapter 3 just now? Why that summer of 1818?

SP: This is when Keats first comes to some terms with what will become his future. George is leaving for America; Tom is deathly ill; and Keats himself will, as if fated, set himself up for his own slow death by pushing his body past its limit on the Northern walking tour with Charles Brown. Bad roads, bad food, bad weather, and worse accommodations will ensure his prolonged sore throat and stomach ailment, so that by the time he returns to London (having completed only half the planned tour) he is extra—vulnerable to the consumption killing Tom, whom he nurses for Tom's three last months in a confined space.

This chapter highlights a dominant motif and fact in the book: the place of brothers or brother surrogates in a man's life. Chapter 3 is about the breakup of literal brothers and the reforming of male relationships for Keats here at the true beginning of his beyond-brief writing career. Brown will move into the center of the picture, but so will the example of Robert Burns, who dies young of drink and poverty, and whose "fame," for Keats, seems extremely compromised. Keats writes—in addition to a lot of letters —quite a few poems on this Northern tour; the one poem he tries to destroy (rescued by Brown) is the "famous" "Sonnet written in the Cottage where Burns was born": the sonnet that begins "This mortal body of a thousand days / Now fills, O Burns, a space in thine own room" and ends "Yet can I drink a bumper to thy name,— / O smile among the shades, for this is fame!"

A fiction writer could not invent a more dramatic, epiphanic example in Keats's life, in which his young past and younger future pour as one into the same moment.

DB: I agree. It sounds like Keats's pivotal period. We all know his sad biography: that he succumbed to tuberculosis at a very early age. He died in a little room in Rome, at twenty-five years and a few months old, on February 23, 1821. Yet we also know from your essay that even by the middle of 1818 he had written, as you say, "nothing . . . that would even suggest immortality, let alone earn it." What happened then?

SP: "Mortality," ironically, is Keats's ultimate subject—mortality placed in tension with "intimations" of its corollary, immortality. That's the major tension between content and form in his work: the perishability of the one against the wishful imperishability of the other. From childhood on, in a kind of mortal progression, everyone close to Keats dies or disappears—father, mother, brother, friends, Fanny Brawne. They die, disappear, while Keats himself becomes more and more invisible. The desire to make him invisible is the real reason he is sent off to Italy. No one knows what to do with him, least of all himself. When Keats comes to some reconciliation with these tensions he begins to write his best, beginning with

"Hyperion: A Fragment," "Eve of St. Agnes," "La Belle Dame," and then the Odes. All written after the Northern tour and Tom's lingering death.

DB: You take your own essay's title from Keats's sonnet, "This Mortal Body of a Thousand Days." His burning desire was to write great poetry, even before he actually did. He saw his forebears in Homer, Milton, Shakespeare, by turns. The present sonnet, addressed to another of his heroes, the Scottish poet Robert Burns, mourns Burns's recent death. Keats raises a toast, "I gulp a bumper to thy name—," and realizes that the price of "fame" is death. To "smile among the shades."

It is eerie to me that Keats wrote "This Mortal Body of a Thousand Days" with about that long to live himself. How much do you think he knew, or foresaw, about his own death? How far could he see? Here in 1818, did he know?

SP: *This* is a question. A good many scholars/biographers pass the thousand days line off as luck—is that the right word? Of course he knew that if he developed any symptoms that there would be a timeline. A thousand is a round number—he doesn't quite make that deadline—he misses it by about a hundred days. I believe it's Tom—to whom he was writing long journal-like letters almost daily from the tour—I believe it's Tom's presence as a sort of ghost in his consciousness that gives him a measure of his own possible future. Keats, on his darker days, is ever the fatalist. George, in effect, is lost; Tom will be; so why not me? Burns's life and death only reinforce this claustrophobia. In a way Keats's posthumous life begins on Ben Nevis, the high and low point of the Northern tour; and his real and best writing life also begins . . . when so much else seems to be ending.

DB: What do you mean by his posthumous life? Maybe this is a good time to talk about the whole book's title, *Posthumous Keats*. These phrases refer to his letter to his great friend (one of those brother surrogates you mention earlier) Charles Brown. In fact, I think this letter is virtually the only thing Keats wrote during those months in Rome before he died. This is the heartbreaking piece where he wrote, about himself, that he had been living a "posthumous existence." How do you see that term working in Keats's mind?

SP: Keats uses the term "posthumous" to refer to his life/existence (he uses at different times both these words) once everyone seems resigned to the fact that—in spite of what is said—his creative and personal life is over and this other, between-life-and-death reality becomes his life, say in the summer of 1820 leading up to his September departure to, arrival in, and four remaining months in Italy.

I, on the other hand, think of and use the term to refer to his afterlife "existence," in which the story of his immortality is played out. The poems and the letters, then, become his posthumous life and he becomes posthumous Keats.

DB: Your essay traces with great detail some of the significant events of that summer. The poet's brother George and his wife, Georgiana, Charles Brown, and others show up. You know what clothes they wore on which days, what routes they traveled to where. You write as though you were there. Did it feel like that?

SP: It's easy to enter into the narrative of Keats's experiences since, through the letters in particular, he provides so much of the vital energy, texture, foreground and background, ups and downs of the living moment. You can only imagine what the real event—internal as well as external—must have been like. And as an observer you might have a totally different view of things; but we get Keats's take almost immediately after the experience, and, sometimes, as if he were "texting" it, we get the experience transformed into language even as it is happening. The Northern tour promotes both of these kinds of transformations: quick memory and on-the-spot. Keats's letters, as we all know, are supreme— none ever better.

DB: His letters are magnificent. In them, for instance, we can follow the great significance of his deep friendships. You pay so much attention to friendship in this essay. Friendship as attention and companionship. Friendship as a kind of love. Friendship as an art form.

SP: Friendship is the chief currency in Keats's world. Keats must have been the best friend you could have: hence, he attracted good people to him. His friend Haslam says, at the end, that if he knows what it is to love he loves John Keats. The only words, other than their names, on John Reynolds's and Charles Brown's tombstones are: Friend of Keats. Friendship—between friends, brothers, and lovers—is what gives life to Keats's letters, both the celebration of it and the complexity of it. Keats is a very moody fellow much of the time; the letters follow his changes, often from paragraph to paragraph. And friendship, in the last year of his life, is what will begin to fail him. What to do with John Keats becomes an unspoken concern among his friends once the TB really takes over and his personality suffers.

DB: Along with the incredible biographical details in this chapter, you fill your essay with equally detailed discussions of Keats's poetry. It's as though I'm reading a biography of the poems themselves. How do you see the relationship between the work and the life of Keats?

SP: The basis for all the biographies of Keats starts with his letters, which suggests that his biography is as much auto- as it is other-biography. Fair copying of his poems becomes his friends' and brothers' job as much as his own. A good portion of Keats's "creative writing" is included in the letters: it is all one flow, just as the shifts in tone and subject within the letters develop as a single consciousness. Truth is, Keats's claim that he would be among the English poets is less hubris than future-think. He died believing he had left "no immortal work behind." Thus all the writing —the sonnets, the romances, the Odes, the quasi-epics—is to him like apprentice work: preparation for what he knew he could do. Life, though, as always, takes over, and *that* becomes the story—not what we planned or wished. Keats's poems are certainly part of his autobiography, especially the autobiography of the imagination.

DB: That certainly counteracts your early training in New Criticism, doesn't it? That's where we learned or were instructed to disengage the life from the work. To treat the work with a kind of clinical objectivity, removed from historical context. Yet what you are doing here is a kind of historicism, mixing biography and cultural context and close reading of the text. Would that be an accurate assessment of your methods?

SP: Yes, exactly. But even the New Critics—and I grew up with them: Brooks and Warren particularly—leave room for the life behind the work. Their interest is in not allowing the life to supersede or supplant the work. They are operating out of modernist assumptions of not permitting the personal to get in the way of the "professional" in the art. To me, the narrative of how Keats's reputation comes about is masterfully compelling, which requires the back-up "narrative" of what that reputation is built on and where, in Severn's fine phrase, the "vicissitudes of his reputation" take us. My own ultimate interest, however, is in the texture of Keats's long posthumous story. A story still continuing.

DB: Toward the end of this chapter, as you mentioned earlier, you recount Keats's ascent of Ben Nevis. Keats was a great walker, like Wordsworth, wasn't he?

SP: Actually Keats was a good walker; Wordsworth and Coleridge great walkers. Keats, finally, is an English Southerner, a city and pastoral walker. His friend Brown was also a great walker. Keats, though, tended toward walking with a purpose, a goal, not for walking's own sake. His ill-fated Northern tour was intended to inspire him to write epic poetry: he was in search of the sublime. The letters to Tom jack up the price of his "inspiring" landscapes—to the point that he tires of them and becomes more interested in the people he meets. The Lake Country and Fingal's Cave are exceptions. Hampstead Heath and the four-mile walk into town (London City): these are his idea of walking.

DB: I suppose there is no way to account for genius, especially for the burst of genius that Keats lived for those months in 1819 writing his great odes. And yet, do you have a theory about how this young, middling sonneteer became the great lyric poet of our language? Or is that the thesis of the whole book?

SP: Yes, that comes close to being one of the central theses of the book: how the Odes, notably, come to be. I will say this: *burst* may not be quite the right metaphor. If you look at the development of Keats's writing from the start—in the more serious poems—and match that development with events in the life, you can see the pattern, or what Henry James calls "the figure in the carpet." The Odes are a product of progress, of building on earlier work; and even the Odes show their own progress, a rising and falling from Psyche to Indolence.

DB: Well, where does the sustained intensity of the Odes come from? They are such phenomenally fine lyric poetry. What evidence or preparation for them do you find in his earlier poems? Does he consider himself already dead in the Odes?

SP: Oh my! This is a question I try to address in my book, but its answer is everywhere in the text of each chapter, sometimes more directly considered than other times. My feeling is—to come to a single point—that Keats invents in the Odes the modern lyric poem, not only through the beauty and intensity of the writing but in the elevation of its achievement to tragic status. He creates the ambition of the modern lyric as a self-reflective medium. Wordsworth's "Tintern Abbey" and Coleridge's conversation poems break the ground for the content of meditation, for the implicit addressing of the muse, but their poems are closer, in feel, to something like "exposition"—and I use this word in its most positivistic sense—and staged drama. For Keats the drama is in the form, not simply the situation. This is why the New Critics loved the Odes—and why, in a wholly different emphasis, Eliot loved Donne.

DB: I have had the pleasure to read the manuscript of *Posthumous Keats*. This third chapter, the present essay, is typical of the biographical detail of the book, and typical of the kind of loving meticulous attention to the poems as well. So far we've been talking about this essay, and book, as though it is an example of biography, a study of the poet John Keats and his circle of friends. But it is much more than that. Honestly, I have never read a book so intimate, so entirely versed in the details and data of the life. The project feels like a confession, or the story of a friendship, or of many friendships.

SP: You keep referring to the Keats book—or at least the chapter in front of you—as an "essay." To me it is a great story, the living story and the story after death, which is another kind of living story: meaning how art, this art, the word on the air, survives, like the breath of the spirit, written down. So it is not just Keats's story; it is the story of poetry, its lyric origins and its lyric destiny. And it is the story of how fragile that destiny is, even, often, accidental. Really how human it is, since nothing is promised, and since what it requires is someone of value paying attention. Poems, for instance, don't automatically go into the canon. Greatness is, more often than not, in disguise.

DB: What do you hope your readers will find in *Posthumous Keats?* Why write this book?

SP: I hope they find the great story that is Keats and that is lyric poetry. I have written this book because I said I would: and why did I—so many years ago—say I would? Because, I guess, the book is about me, too.

DB: Yes, it is. I know you have a long history of preparation for this book. Did you study him in graduate school? I know you have read all the biographies, the critical studies, and you have utterly absorbed the poems. But my guess is that you have also personally followed his pathways in England and Italy, too, literally walked his paths, looked over the bay in Naples, climbed Ben Nevis. Is that right?

SP: I studied with one old Romantic English scholar who had a lot to do with securing the status of the Keats-Shelley House in Rome. His name is Neville Rogers. I have visited every single place in the Keats story. I spent a year, almost every day, at the Keats House in Hampstead—before it became such a public place: the Keats Library at the Keats House. And I have spent a lot of time at the Keats-Shelley House in Rome; in fact, I stayed on the floor above Keats's and Severn's rooms for a few nights—a very strange experience. I didn't get a lot of sleep, since the Spanish Steps are an ongoing meeting place. I've "walked"—by car—the trip from Naples to Rome; I've climbed Ben Nevis; and I've trailed along much of the journey north that Keats and Brown traveled that fateful summer. There is no substitute, whatever the subject, for being there.

DB: In this whole project, what surprised you most? What did you learn?

SP: What surprised me most is the human vulnerability in everything we touch. And what I learned most is how much I love prose.

DB: That's really interesting. Do you mean how much you love writing prose? What is the basis for that feeling? Prose's elegance, or its capability to carry and sustain a story? Or something else entirely?

SP: I guess I *do* mean writing it, writing prose—writing, I hope, in the spirit of Pound's dictum that poetry should be at least as well written as good prose: or, to turn it around, that prose should be at least as well written as good poetry. You're asking, in addition, about differences and similarities between poetry and prose. The truth is, I think, that they are entirely different, if for no other reason than that they express, condition, acquire different contents—they create different contents. Critics will sometimes laud a piece of prose for its "poetic" qualities; no one ever praises poetry for its "prosaic" distinctions. I guess both means are roundish: and tasty: but they really are apples and oranges.

The other thing is that prose offers spatial and temporal options that counter, in poetry, certain energies. Poetry pulls in, includes by selection; prose reaches out, embraces its choices. Style is a term we use for prose; form is the term for poetry. Faulkner and Hemingway represent "opposing" styles, as do Proust and Flaubert. (I do wish poetry critics would stop using the word "style" to talk about formal differences in poets. It's a kind of failure of imagination to not find a more on-the-money term.) I love the lengths I can go to in prose; I love the meander, the wander, the walkability of prose; I love its territory. Perhaps this is a function of age: all that memory and experience backed up behind what needs to be said.

DB: Keats is not just the subject of this prose project. He is a subject of several of your finest poems. If my guess is right, your first poem in which he appears is "Posthumous Keats." That poem appears in your 1984 collection *Summer Celestial*. Along with the majestic title poem, "Posthumous Keats" is unlike any of your previous poems—so directly and fully a portrait-sketch of the poet and his friend Joseph Severn.

SP: This "project" all started with the "Posthumous Keats" poem, and my realization that certain connections in his story had not been made, and that the story itself was overwhelming in its richness, its "light and shade." My other Keatsian poems are responses to moments and details in the life, as if, perhaps, they were my own experience.

DB: It also seems to me that your capability to find space for Keats in your poems has extended to other figures. Whitman, Wordsworth, Whistler. And in your new book, an even wider cast of characters appears—from Lyndon Johnson to Gene Tierney, your dear friend Bill Matthews to Audubon, Eliot, Dickinson, and so many other acquaintances, influences, and neighbors. It's like a big family gathering. Does it feel like that to you? It is also like a life-list, everyone accumulated, tallied, and accounted for.

SP: I guess, for me, these other figures are compelling because they draw something out in me: an identification, of course, but also a sort of forgiveness of self, which applies even to Bill Matthews. People we love or respond to have that gift for naming something in us and making us know it.

DB: It's fascinating to me how your books of poetry have grown over the years. I mean this in three ways. First, your later books are bigger. The first few were, as they say, slender volumes, and the poems there are tight, even meticulous lyrics, spare in their rhetoric and song. And the subjects are closely managed in those first books—natural descriptions, and a few fundamental narratives of the mother and father. *Out-of-the-Body Travel* and *Summer Celestial* are a son's books. Yet in *Boy on the Step* and *The Marriage in the Trees,* your palette deepens: more poems, more space, and more people. Neighbors, lovers, friends.

Now you have finished a new manuscript, your first collection of all-new poems since 1996 and *The Marriage in the Trees. Old Heart*—which Norton will release this fall—is your biggest book. It has the most poems, the most pages. It also has the most people. It is not a son's book. It is, in some way, a father's book, though you have no children. This is the conundrum of "Paraphrase of the Parable of the Prodigal Son," isn't it, which ends with "He will die, / like many of us, without children."

SP: My first two books were apprentice books, tryings-out. I never had a teacher, as such, for poetry writing. I taught myself by studying whom I considered to be the masters, especially the Romantics and Moderns, and especially English models. Thus I have never quite got over the feeling that I sound, constantly, old-fashioned as a lyric poet—indeed, fearful that being a "lyric" poet somehow is a way of being excused. *Out-of-the-Body Travel* is when I found my voice and a sense of direction; found a way of admitting the silences and the spaces in-between things in my poems. The way my poems have "grown" in size and consciousness is exactly how I, as a person, have grown. The next poems, after *Old Heart,* will be that much more accepting, and, I hope, large hearted. There is no substitute for honesty—it changes everything and frees you of the hold of "dark matter."

DB: *Old Heart* is also profoundly a friend's book. There are your students here, and their own parents and children. There are poems to your friend Bill Matthews. And more neighbors, townspeople, movie stars, painters, and pals.

Many poets' worlds shrink as they grow through middle age. Yours has become more inclusive. And the poems themselves grow more formally spacious and various. How do you find the right form for a poem? Do you start with syllabics? Or a line? Or a story?

SP: To me, the heartbeat in my poems is syllabic but with an accent that I hope is natural and inherent within the language of the line and the sentence. You have to hear the language, word by word; otherwise, the writing degenerates into the noise of only-narrative, like a book report of autobiography. The seeing in a poem is in the hearing. The hearing is all the page has: everything else flows from that. If you get the hearing right, then you have a chance to say something of value that will be heard. The hearing has visual qualities, too—the right rhythm enlarges the space and helps find the form.

DB: Your Keats book is a book about mortality and immortality. So is *Old Heart*. Your own brush with heart trouble a few years ago underlines every other subject here—heart trouble as cardiac failure, heart trouble as the erotic life, heart trouble as the vexed life and death of friendship and passion.

SP: This is probably true for all of us: that our lifespan is somewhere between the mortalities of our parents. I have, as of today, outlived the death date of my father by twelve years; and I have ten more years left before I reach the death date of my mother. Both died of heart attacks. My own heart attacks reminded me of this inheritance. And yes, there is that other kind of heart trouble: love and its ablutions. There's no solving love or absolving it. There's just living through it. Friendship is love without sex. Sex also changes everything.

Arthur Sze

MARIANA COOK

ARTHUR SZE was born in New York City in 1950 and graduated from the University of California, Berkeley, as a Phi Beta Kappa with a self-designed major. He has conducted poetry residencies and taught widely in the United States, and recently retired after twenty-two years of teaching at the Institute of American Indian Arts in Santa Fe, New Mexico, where he also served as the city's first poet laureate and where he continues to life with his wife, the poet Carol Moldaw, and their daughter, Sarah.

Arthur Sze is the author of eight books of poetry, including most recently *The Ginkgo Light,* (2009), *Quipu* (2005), *The Redshifting Web: Poems 1970–1998* (1998), and *Archipelago* (1995), each from Copper Canyon Press. His individual poems have appeared widely in such journals as *American Poetry Review, Boston Review, Conjunctions,* the *Kenyon Review,* the *Paris Review,* the *New Yorker,* and *Virginia Quarterly Review,* and have been translated into Albanian, Bosnian, Chinese, Dutch, Italian, Romanian, Spanish, and Turkish. A second-generation Chinese American,

Sze is also a celebrated translator of Chinese poetry. His *The Silk Dragon: Translations from the Chinese* was published in 2001 by Copper Canyon Press. He is the editor of a newly released anthology, *Chinese Writers on Writing*, from Trinity University Press.

For his work Sze has been widely honored. He is recipient of a PEN Southwest Book Award for poetry, a Lila Wallace-Reader's Digest Writers' Award, a Guggenheim Fellowship, an American Book Award, a Lannan Literary Award for Poetry, two National Endowment for the Arts Creative Writing fellowships, as well as a George A. and Eliza Gardner Howard Foundation Fellowship, three grants from the Witter Bynner Foundation for Poetry, and a Western States Book Award for Translation.

After a New Moon

Each evening you gaze in the southwest sky
as a crescent extends in argentine light.
When the moon was new, your mind was
desireless, but now both wax to the world.
While your neighbor's field is cleared,
your corner plot is strewn with dessicated
sunflower stalks. You scrutinize the bare
apricot limbs that have never set fruit,
the wisteria that has never blossomed;
and wince, hearing how, at New Year's,
teens bashed in a door and clubbed strangers.
Near a pond, someone kicks a dog out
of a pickup. Each second, a river edged
with ice shifts course. Last summer's
exposed tractor tire is nearly buried
under silt. An owl lifts from a poplar,
while the moon, no, the human mind
moves from brightest bright to darkest dark.

Returning to Northern New Mexico after a Trip to Asia

A tea master examines pellets with tweezers,
points to the varying hues then pushes
the dish aside. At another shop, a woman
rinses a cylindrical cup with black tea:
we inhale, nod, sip from a second cup—
rabbit tracks in snow become tracks
in my mind. At a banquet, I eat something
sausage-like, am told "It's a chicken's ball."
Two horses huddle under leafless poplars.
A neighbor runs water into an oval container,
but, in a day, the roan bangs it with his hoof.
The skunks and raccoons have vanished.
What happened to the *End World Hunger* project?
Revolutionary slogans sandblasted off
Anhui walls left faint outlines. When
wind swayed the fragrant pine branches
in a Taiwan garden, Sylvie winced, "Kamikaze
pilots drank and whored their last nights here."

Spectral Line

1.

Who passes through the gates of the four directions?
Robin coughs as she tightens a girth, adjusts saddle,
and, leading Paparazzo past three stalls, becomes
woman-leading-horse-into-daylight. Though the Chu
army conquered, how long does a victory last?
The mind sets sliver to sliver to comprehend, spark;
the mind tessellates to bring into being a new shape.
When the Blackfeet architect unveiled his master plan
with a spirit way leading to a center that opened
to the four directions, I saw the approach to
the Ming Tombs, with pairs of seated then standing
lions, camels, elephants, horses lining the way.
I snapped when, through the camera lens,
I spotted blue sneakers—but not the woman—protruding
from the sides of a seated horse, and snapped
a white-haired woman with bound feet munching fry bread.
Peripheral details brighten like mating fireflies.
Then Gloria pointed to the east, gasped,
"Navajos will never set foot here: you've placed
these buildings in the ceremonial form of a rattlesnake."

2.

Blinking red light on the machine: he presses
the button, and a voice staggers, "I'm back,"

"I don't know where I am," "I drive but can't
recollect how I get to where I am,"—whiteout

when a narwhal sprays out its blowhole and water
crystallizes in air—"Thirty-three days,"

he presses replay: the voice spirals, "I lost
four members of my family in a whaling accident";

he writes down numbers, 424–0590, dials,
"My cousin killed himself after his girlfriend

killed herself," richochets in his ears; though
the name is blurred, he guesses at bowhead

ribs in a backyard, canisters of radioactive
waste stored inland on Saint Lawrence Island;

twenty below: Yupik children play string games;
when he broke the seal on a jar of smoked

king salmon, he recalled his skin and clothes
reeked of smoke from the float house woodstove.

3.

The stillness of heart-shaped leaves breaks
when a grasshopper leaps. I have never
watched so many inch along branches before.
Though they have devastated butterfly bushes,
they have left these lilacs unscathed, but can I
shrug, be marathoner-running-into-spring-light-
over-piñon-dotted-hills? The mind may snag,
still, weigh, sift, incubate, unbalance,
spark, rebalance, mend, release; when one
neighbor cuts grasses infested with grasshoppers,
inadvertently drives them into another's
organic farm loaded with beets, lettuce, basil,
carrots, kale, chard: we cannot act as if
we were asleep, do not entrench boundaries
but work to dissolve them. From light to dark
is a pass of how many miles? Together they sowed
dark millet and reclaimed the reed marsh.
As we entwine in darkness-beginning-to-trace-
light, dew evaporates off tips of grasses.

4.

North they headed to Water Bend, what joy awaited them?

"I had to shoot myself or shoot someone else";

cries of snow geese in the wave of sunrise;

the secretary winked, "I'm wearing edible panties";

concubines were immolated on the emperor's death;

the green tips of a leafing apple;

"Here are instructions for when I am dead";

he was retracing the Long Walk;

when we addressed them as *tongzhi,* comrades, they laughed;

she swallowed the white sleeping pills and nearly ODed;

the spring wind blew the ax off the chopping block;

when confronted with plagiarized lines, he shrugged, "I dreamed them";

the ex-marine checked staff desks at 8:20 for attendance;

from the south, elephants; from the west, horses; from the north, camels;

stepping through the miniature garden, they had no idea
they were writing the character "heart";

she danced in a topless bar;

when the army recruiting film previewed in the underground bomb
          shelter,
the crowd jeered;

she surprised him with a jar of Labrador leaves;

"Try to add to the sum total of human culture";

though the edges and angles are many, who knows their number?

5.

Acoma Pueblo,
Diné,
Crow,
Oglala Lakota,
Menominee,
Northern Ute,
Zuni Pueblo,
Kiowa,
Muckleshoot,
Standing Rock Lakota,
Muscogee,
Ojibwe,
San Ildefonso Pueblo,
Comanche,
Tlingit,
Mescalero Apache,
Siberian Yupik,
Jemez Pueblo,
Pawnee,
Chugach/Alutiiq,
Mohawk,
Swampy Cree,
Osage,
Taos Pueblo,
Arapaho,
Jicarilla Apache,
Paiute,
Haida,
Onandaga,
Cochiti Pueblo,
Sioux,

Eastern Shawnee,
Caddo,
Santa Clara,
Northern Cheyenne,
Prairie Band Potawatomi,
Choctaw,
Chickasaw,
Tsalagi,
Inupiat.

6.

We forage for black and yellow morels
under tulip poplars, but they are camouflaged
on the forest floor. Wherever I squint,
I mark varicolored leaves, clusters of deer scat;
at first I zigzag a branch back and forth
under leaves, expecting to uncover some,
then learn to spot-check near the trunks,
forage further out above the roots among
lichened rocks. We bring two dozen back,
sauté them, add to pasta, salad; sip wine;
but what coalesces in the body for weeks
are glimpses of blossoming redbuds while
driving along a road; horses by the second gate;
lights on the porch; a basket of apples,
bread, farm milk set at a downstairs table;
rocking horse upstairs; two tapers lit;
quicksilver kisses, a diamond light; and,
before, tremor when you felt something odd:
pulled a black tick off from behind your ear,
brushed a smaller one out of your hair.

7.

Who rescues hunters tipped into arctic waters?
The hour is a cashmere scarf; as a black man

near a fountain raises saxophone to his lips
and showers the street with shimmering gold,

red lights of an ambulance weaving in traffic
bob into distance. From a dome, a pendulum

swings, almost touches numbers that mark
the hours in a circle on the floor. When

Robin's coworkers were terminated, she left
her telecommunications job to groom the horses

she loves, even in zero degree weather; she
cinches a saddle on Nemo even now. A meadow

mushroom, covered overnight under a glass bowl,
releases, onto white paper, a galaxy of

chocolate-brown spores. When you are still,
you spot the chance tracks of the living.

Who can suspend time on a string, make it
arc back and forth while earth rotates around it?

8.

Incoming freshmen have been taken hostage,
the letter to the president began; we demand
computers and art supplies; limo service
to the Gathering of Nations; the sum total
of Pell Funds be released at once. Benildus Hall
is our headquarters. When the SWAT team
surrounded the building, someone pointed
to the small print: *Happy April First.*
The mind seizes a spore then releases it.
Descending into the Ming Tomb, I discerned
electric lights; a cold, iron railing;
people shuffling down stairs; camera flashes;

people shuffling across, up the other side,
then out; but nothing was at the center;
only now—the moment when water from six
directions is water from the six directions.
A neighbor listens for wings before dawn;
plums begin to begin to drop from branches.

9.

"A driver's door opened, and a head rolled
out of the burning car"—once she told me,

I could not expunge it. A backhoe beeps
when the driver moves it into reverse, beeps

above the din of morning traffic. A ginkgo
flames into yellow-gold, while, elsewhere,

red tulips flare on a slope. The mind weighs,
balances antinomies: at graduation, a student

speaker carries a black bag to the podium,
unveils bow, arrows, his entire body shaking,

and threatens to take aim at board members—
dissolves into air; a student in the audience

who slurs "far out" after every sentence
dissolves into air; the man who wafts eagle

feather above head, shoulders, along arms,
onto palms—dissolves into air; singers and

drummers who start and end dissolve into air;
and stillness, as we stir to dawn light, breaks.

Demolishing Hierarchy

A Conversation with Arthur Sze

David Baker: I've been a fan of your work for a long time, as you know, Arthur. For our conversation, I think we'll start with these two new poems, but we'll also reach back into the archives to talk about others of your poems that we printed in the *Kenyon Review* over the past several years.

I'm drawn to the powerful paradox that these two poems create, each in its way. First, I am attracted to the sharply chiseled shape of the poems. "After a New Moon" and "Returning to Northern New Mexico after a Trip to Asia" both commence with lines that feel almost like blank verse. Or perhaps they are loosely accentual, with four and sometimes five strong beats to each line. And the lines are shapely and balanced.

The paradox arises, then, when the coherence of the lineation meets the very quick-changing narrative, the dramatic or cognitive sense of things. The poems make such surprising turns. They change pronouns, they change locations, they change their patterns of image. These shifts occur almost with each new sentence. I find the tension between formality and surprise, then, to be powerful and evocative. How much of these tactics is willed, and how much is discovered or happened upon?

Arthur Sze: I like to think of my writing process as a zigzag way. I often start with slivers, fragments, and try to germinate phrases and nurture the process of discovery. It's important not to know too soon where it's going —it's important to encourage and even sustain this process of suspense— but, eventually, I have so many phrases I start sifting and searching for what has urgency, what feels most alive. As I do this, I find I'm also searching for an arc, a structure, and a form begins to take shape. As I start orchestrating some of the slivers, I have a conscious tactic of writing the phrases out in two-line stanzas, where the white spaces enable me to leap more freely.

I wouldn't call these two-line stanzas couplets, because, to my mind, a couplet has a kind of integrity, whereas, in this early stage, I'm playing more with juxtaposition of phrasing and trying to keep open, in the white space, the possibility of leaping into something unexpected, or shifting tonally into another register, or, alternately, developing a narrative line that might fill in the space with a greater sense of completion. So even after I have a provisional shape to the poem, I still go back and forth between what I like to call "rigor" (inner necessity) and "spontaneity" (the possibility of discovery and surprise). Eventually, I hope to have a poem that harnesses both.

For the two poems you mention, I checked first drafts and found that in "After a New Moon," only one phrase from the first sheet of phrases, "the shifting course of a river," eventually made it, in slightly different form, into the final poem. In "Returning to Northern New Mexico after a Trip to Asia," the last phrase, starting with "Kamikaze pilots," was there at the outset, but I tried repeatedly in the early stages to make it the opening. I eventually realized it was much more effective as the end. I mention the specific genesis to these two poems, because they show how the full poem is rarely there at the outset and how the tension between formality and surprise has to be earned.

DB: What do you mean "the first sheet of phrases"? You say you start with slivers and fragments. I think of Emerson's evocative statement in "The Poet" that "bare lists of words are found suggestive to an imaginative and excited mind." Is that how these poems started, as phrases and lists, in two-line groups? Do you also start with random sentences? Or something else entirely, like a sense of music or of graphic arrangement?

AS: The two poems grew in different ways. In "After a New Moon," I started with a vague pressure and wrote out a series of phrases in two-line groups. I wouldn't call them lists, because there wasn't any verticality to them. Rather, the phrases were more like charged clusters. I agree with Emerson's statement and would expand "bare lists" to "bare lists and phrases." I often play with random phrases with the feeling that they're somehow connected below surface in ways I can't see. Sometimes a sense of music propels a phrase forward, sometimes I search for a sense of line. It's a highly intuitive process. In "Returning to Northern New Mexico after a Trip to Asia," I had the last two lines very quickly and, with it, a sense of cadence and line. I also had a clear narrative impulse but pursued several narrative threads before they coalesced.

DB: Your poems—and these two are typical of this technique—frequently have a narrative coherence to them. Yet they are not stories exactly, nor do they proceed in a linear narrative. So what determines the order of the phrases and pieces? Even if the effect is of the random or the concurrent, still you are making decisions about sequence on the page.

AS: Sequencing is very important. At a certain stage, if I feel I'm in too much control, I might take a series of phrases, even the beginning and ending, and reverse their order to see if I can discover something unforeseen. Eventually, when I work out the final sequencing to a poem, I'm searching for a quality of inevitable unfolding: although there's no linear narrative, I need to feel each twist and turn is essential.

DB: The effect of shifting, of shifting phrases, as well as changing scene or image or focus, becomes part of the speaker's own self-awareness in these poems. But more so, it becomes part of his storytelling tactic. At the end of "After a New Moon" he revises himself, as if even he is surprised by the direction of thinking in his poem. It's the moon—no, it's his mind that moves from bright to dark.

Is this a form of complicity on his part, of desiring to come closer to us? Is this revision, which you have kept in the poem rather than edited out, an indication of the provisional nature of things?

AS: I believe the interruption in the next-to-last line of "After a New Moon" has several effects. First, I want to say that the disparity between intention and effect is one of the great mysteries of art. I can have an intention, or set of intentions, but the effect, or cluster of effects, may be quite different from what I expected. And that's good: a poem is often smarter than the poet. Just as the process of creation involves exercising control and releasing it, so the effects in a poem are often more powerful when they are least anticipated.

Here I want to add a distinction between superficial and deep surprise. On a first reading, a poem may dazzle with surface effects, but if the underlying rigor isn't there, the initial surprises evaporate, whereas, with a deep surprise, there may be an initial feeling of discomfort and disorientation, but over several readings, the singularity of vision and underlying rigor emerge. In this case, the surprise becomes powerful and lasting.

In creating "After a New Moon," I happened to catch the speaker in the act of asserting then revising the assertion even as he makes it. As you mention, I could have edited it out, but, instead, I felt it was what the Greeks called a *hermaion,* a gift, a lucky find. In doing so, I hoped to enact the process of qualification and discovery, rather than present the result.

I was also consciously working with a voice casting a spell, and, yes, I hoped this interruption would reveal the provisional nature of not just this assertion but of all things. The notion that this is a form of complicity, or desiring to come closer to the reader, is an important element to that rupture, but it wasn't, at least in the act of writing it, my primary concern.

Nevertheless, as an unforeseen or unanticipated effect, it's a significant one.

DB: More about the provisional then. I notice and am moved by the constant flux of your poems. Nothing holds still and yet a kind of abiding peace or acceptance grows, even when the details of a poem are grim or hard. How do you think about the relation of stability to change or the provisional?

AS: I like to invoke the image of the yin/yang symbol, where, in the swirl of white, there's a black point, and, in the swirl of black, there's a white point. Darkness isn't privileged over light, and light isn't privileged over dark. Rather, the visible points inside of each swirl are the points of interconnection and transformation. I want to be paradoxically rooted in the flux of the world, and I'm drawn to the points and to the edge where light turns into dark, and dark into light. As part of this process, I'm interested in demolishing hierarchy: a butterfly opening its wings may be of equal importance as the death of a friend in a car crash. And I like to utilize equivocal contrast as a means to heighten the tension between antinomial forces and give shape to the flux.

DB: Demolishing hierarchy. Yes, I think that's a primary aesthetic (and probably political) impulse in your poems. I want to return to that in a little while when we look at some of your longer poems, where the effect is even more vividly felt.

But I notice another important shared characteristic in the poems at hand. That is, their quality of after-effect. Both poems are uttered "after" an event or trip. I don't notice this trope as a frequent one in your other short poems, so I wonder if it's a new thing, or perhaps a coincidence.

The effect, though, is a powerful one. The poems come to us with a kind of gathered wisdom or a sense of experience. Something has happened and now the speaker can report. The world seems fresh, too, in each poem's after-effect—things seen with an especially clear light, whether those things are beautiful or difficult.

AS: I think the conscious harnessing of an after-effect in these two poems is new. "Returning to Northern New Mexico" was written before "After a New Moon."

Some background might be pertinent here. In November 2007, I was in Hualien, Taiwan, for an international poetry festival that was held in a pine garden retreat. As I looked out toward the Pacific Ocean, the idyllic scene was demolished when Sylvie Tang, a graduate student who assisted me as a translator, told me Kamikaze pilots spent their last days there, drinking and whoring, before launching themselves against American naval warships.

That jolt became a seed for the poem. And, when I finished "Returning to New Mexico," I felt the trope of an after-shock could be developed more figuratively. As I worked on "After a New Moon," the interruption in the next-to-last line created the shock that reverberated through the poem. Because the two poems are each eighteen lines long, were written consecutively, deal with similar issues, even if in contrasting ways, I think of them as twins.

DB: I do, too. But there are a couple of interesting differences. In "After a New Moon" the second-person point of view also suggests an "I," a surrogate for the speaker. That's clearly the camera angle of the poem. In "Returning to Northern New Mexico" the stance is explicitly first person. And yet the mood and mindset of the two poems seem pretty similar. How do you think of the differences there in pronoun and point of view?

AS: I often play with shifting pronouns and point of view and believe that's part of the destabilizing and provisional nature of things. It's also a rich arena for creative exploration. In "After a New Moon," I hope the "you" is rich in ambiguity. It could be the unnamed "I" is addressing an other, a spouse, for instance, or the unnamed speaker could be addressing and struggling with an aspect of himself. If the speaker is struggling with an aspect of himself, it's possible the "I" becomes changed in the process.

DB: In your most recent previous *Kenyon Review* appearance, we printed your longer poem "Spectral Line." I think of this as one of your central recent poems. It also seems like a mini-anthology of your primary methods. These methods are compressed in "After a New Moon" and "Returning to Northern New Mexico." In "Spectral Line," with its nine sections, they are more extended.

From the first section you show your ability to combine and juxtapose —from Native American references to Buddhist sensibilities to personal and domestic narratives. As the poem proceeds, I find changes in pronoun and point of view, in stanza structure, even in a kind of syntactic method. The poem moves quickly, as in part two, then seems suspended in meditation and peacefulness, as in part three.

AS: The scientific definition of "Spectral Line" is, in small scale, a chromatic fingerprint of an excited gas, and, in large scale, a band of images corresponding to radiation emitted by a particular source. When I wrote "Spectral Line," the Institute of American Indian Arts was my source of energy, and I wanted to use the scientific meanings as an underlying, structural principle; but I was also interested in the idea of a specter haunting the imagination.

I love working in sequences, where there's room to create worlds inside the world of the poem. And I like the large-scale rhythmical possibilities a sequence affords. Section two enacts a disorienting experience of loss and needs to jar and move quickly, whereas, in section three, as you note, there's a floating stillness. In orchestrating a sequence, I'm consciously working with stillness and motion, a variety of diction and syntax, braiding narratives.

DB: One of the critical sections is section four. This is where you rip apart the syntax, suspend a need for closure, and let the stanzas hang there, connected by the mere staple of a semicolon. They aren't really stanzas, are they?

What I mean is each segment feels equivalent to each other, each is like a segment in a collage, and the effect is a kind of concurrent happening. You manage to create a feeling of nonjudgment, of equanimity or acceptance—from the near-suicide to the spring apple, from the flirty secretary to the grandeur of adding to "human culture." And you end with a question. The feeling of equanimity or equivalence is important to you, isn't it? So is the resistance to closure.

AS: Yes, section four isn't really organized into stanzas. I like that you call the phrases segments. They aren't quite fragments—many are syntactically complete sentences—but they are juxtaposed to create a kind of simultaneity where linear time and consequence are suspended: It's as if anything can happen, or all things happen at once. I'm interested in incorporating a wide range of experience and creating a vast web of equivalences. A feeling of equanimity comes from a kind of release, of nonattachment, but if there was only equanimity, there would be no poem. And, yes, I'm interested in resisting closure. Instead of circling back and closing things off, I've noticed that my poems often expand, rest, then expand more, or they stop on a dime. In an earlier time, the closure of the poem may have been satisfying, but, in our world today, closure risks a premature or false sense of completion.

DB: Why do you think we resist closure these days, or, as you say, a sense of completion? Is it our modernist inheritance, our distrust of the complete, our distrust of authority? Must the vase have a crack in it?

AS: I think closure represents a kind of closing off, and, with the increasing complexities of our contemporary world, it's harder and harder to do. Closure, I think, is like the answer to a question. If someone asks a question and you can make an authoritative answer, you attain a sense of completion; but, if the answer is provisional and leads to another question, then the authority of the answer is undermined.

It is easier to employ closure if you have a linear narrative: x leads to y and eventually z is a kind of denouement. But what if the world is a ten-dimensional game of go? [Go is the Japanese name—in Chinese, it's called *weiqi*—where two players, alternately, place black stones or white stones on a board of crisscrossed lines and attempt to capture each other's stones by surrounding them.] If causes and effects are unseen and unclear, and a vast web is in place instead of a billiard ball view of causality, closure, completion is virtually impossible. So resistance to closure, I think, has a bit of all that you mention: modernist inheritance, distrust of the complete, distrust of authority.

I would add that my experience of the world is closer to simultaneity and to *weiqi* than to linear narration. Nevertheless, if someone asserts that the vase *must* have a crack in it, I have to object. Poetry must resist any form of coercion. If the prevailing mode is so far in the direction of open forms and resistance to closure, then it become interesting to break expectation and consider whether a new kind of closure is possible. In addition, I think there's also an issue about the self and ego of the artist. In Western literature, the ending to the *Divine Comedy* is an immense form of closure. It's thrilling to get to the end of the journey and experience "the love which moves the sun and the other stars." All of the cosmos is put into place, and Dante has supreme confidence in himself; but when the self is fractured and decentered, as it is, it's, again, virtually impossible to attain completion, and completion itself may not even be a goal.

DB: Section five is an even more concrete section. Emerson again: we have here a "bare list" of Native American tribes. Names like a roll call. This is the center section of the poem, midpoint. I know about your years of teaching at the Institute of American Indian Arts in Santa Fe. Are these tribes a representation of some of your past students' backgrounds? What's the desired effect here?

AS: I wrote "Spectral Line" during my last year of teaching at the Institute of American Indian Arts, and section five is indeed a roll call. At graduation each year, it is customary for students to be called on stage to receive their diploma, and their tribal affiliations follow their names. During the twenty-two years I taught at IAIA, I worked with students from, probably, two hundred tribes across the United States. Looking back, I thought of students who stood out, and, instead of their names, I used their tribes.

Many sections in "Spectral Line" leap and move with restless energy, but, at the center of this poem, I wanted to stop making large leaps and create some relative stillness. As the names of tribes are articulated, I wanted the naming to foreground the texture of sounds and for everything else to drop away. From an epistemological point of view, the roll call embodies the one and the many. All of the names are names of Native American tribes, yet, within that one, there's infinite variety.

DB: There is so much searching and hunting in the poem. For mushrooms, for names, for lovers, for knowledge, for meaningful ritual. And yet the poem also asserts that "nothing was at the center." That feels like the poem's truest discovery. Pieces, stories, the vulgar and the sublime together, and yet we don't find a center or a meaning so much as we find, well, the going-on of things—the provisional again—and the poem is about that going-on-ness, an acceptance of it. Is that a reasonable reading?

AS: Yes, though I think "nothing was at the center" may be misconstrued. From a Western perspective, "nothing" may appear to be a blank and feel disappointing; but from an Eastern perspective, there's a charged poetics of emptiness. For instance, here's a rough paraphrase of chapter 11, from the *Dao De Jing:* "thirty spokes converge upon a single hub, but it is the hole in the center that enables the wheel and cart to move. You make a bowl from clay, but the empty space makes it useful. You make doors and windows for a room, but the empty space makes it livable. While the tangible has advantages, it is emptiness that makes it useful." In this light, the "nothing at the center" is thrilling and is the beginning of all creative possibility.

To come back to "Spectral Line," in section eight, when the speaker discovers the "nothing" at the center of things, he is discovering the source of all creation. In Stevens's world, it's where the imagination finds "what will suffice." In Yeats's world, it's where he writes, "Come near, come near, come near—Ah, leave me still / A little space for the rose-breath to fill!"

DB: That's wonderful—the positive aesthetic of the nothing. Silence as the perfect poetic.

Let me turn back further now to some of your earlier work. In 2003 we published your poem "Didyma." It's another poem that I think is central in your work. You included it in your 2005 book *Quipu*.

You explain in a note to this book that quipus are textiles and are found in old Asian as well as Incan cultures. They are a series of knotted cords used to keep records and make calculations and maybe tell stories. They are dyed strings, and they are "read" by the hands as well as eyes, is that right? They seem to me essentially a form of memory.

AS: I hesitate to call quipus textiles, because textiles usually implies woven fiber or fiber used in weaving. Merriam-Webster's defines a quipu as "a device made of a main cord with smaller varicolored cords attached and knotted and used by the ancient Peruvians (as for calculating)."

They are indeed a series of dyed, knotted cords, and it's important to distinguish numerical from nonnumerical quipus. Numerical quipus employ different kinds of knots that encode the numbers one through nine, and the knots are placed at positions following a base-ten system. So numerical quipus are recording devices: They might show the amount of potatoes, even the kinds of potatoes, in storage, which would be crucial information during a famine. Nonnumerical quipus, however, are believed to encode language. There's a historical account of an Inca runner who arrives at a village and, after he holds up the quipu, the indigenous people join a revolt against the Spanish. That account supports the thesis that quipus can also convey narrative information. In either case, the strings are "read" by the hands as well as eyes, and memory is an important factor.

DB: The quipu provides a useful analog for your poems. Tactile as well as textual, sensual, primitive, and again, possessed of a kind of equivalent representative system. Quipus are metaphors that don't make preferences as much as they make connections. And your poems connect things like science and ritual, the personal and the political, the organic and the synthetic; and, of course, your poems cross-reference so many cultures. Asian and Native American and Western and contemporary and ancient. Do you think of your poems, especially these longer sequences, as quipus?

AS: I conceived of the book *Quipu* (2005) as one large quipu, and the title poem, "Quipu," as one extended sequence inside of the larger one. In that book, I thought of language as fiber and deliberately worked with different forms of knotting. For instance, the repetitions of knotting can be seen in anaphora and epiphora. In the title poem, I used the word "as" many times but employed the dictionary's eleven different meanings so that the repetitions are elegant variations and layer the poem; but I don't think of my other sequences as quipus. Instead, they use a great variety of other structures or models.

DB: What are some of the other primary models for your poetry?

AS: I've used a variety of structures for my sequences. "Archipelago" braids the experience of a Zen garden with a Native American ceremony; "The String Diamond" utilizes the structure of go; "Earthshine" utilizes astronomy; "Six Persimmons" is an ekphrastic and is inspired by the eponymous painting; "Before Completion" draws on the divination text, the *Yijing*.

I've also created my own models. After I wrote many sectional sequences, Carol suggested that I try to write a sustained poem with a different model. I decided to open up the tercet form into a 1–2–2–1 form with indeterminate length. This model felt appropriate as a meditative space, and I created several poems using that form.

DB: Let's talk more about the poem. Didyma is an ancient Greek temple, though its location is in present-day Turkey. It ranked just below Delphi as the most important oracle sanctuary in the Hellenic world. So here you are working with another cultural narrative and tracing the structures of memory and vision.

Like "Spectral Line," your poem "Didyma" is a sectional poem. Some of the sections are tight, with rather linear narratives, while some are splayed with voices, pieces, tidbits, the found as well as the made. There's another wanderer here, a searcher, in part one, and in parts two and four we hear again the interplay of voices and images—pieces of disparate scenes—connected with semicolons. It's tempting to hear one voice as commenting on the previous, but it's also tempting to see the pieces are interchangeable and movable.

Was this poem written in a manner similar to "Spectral Line?"

AS: There are some similarities, but there are also important differences. Both sequences are grounded in a specific place, but, at Didyma, I experienced a crucial moment, which is part of its architectural design. Before reaching the inner sanctum, Carol and I walked down a dark and narrow vaulted ramp. The passage is long enough that your eyes adjust to the dark, but then you step out into sunlight and are literally dazzled. That intensely physical moment was also, for me, the experience of love, and I wrote that section first. From the compositional order, sections 8, 3, 4, 2, 1, 5, 6, 7, 9, 10, you can see that I had the end just before the expansive ending right at the outset. In "Spectral Line," however, I started with segments, section 4, and tried to create a microcosm or small signature of bands inside of what I knew would eventually be a much larger poem.

DB: The center of the poem, part five, comments on its own procedure: "A point of exhaustion can become a point of renewal." At this point the poem pauses, then opens into a more personal narrative. Your daughter appears, and the poem's location is clarified: a family trip to the Dardanelles and Black Sea—that is, a contemporary scene near the temple of Didyma. And so once more your poem becomes a series of layers, like a palimpsest. A thickly textured and richly historied scene. A mural. Section seven remains one of my favorite pieces of all your poems. It is a chant as much as a poem. I remember hearing you read "Didyma" years ago, and this section still haunts me. As you read it, you seemed to measure the time with your hands. Each segment was weighted and balanced, with the same amount of time as the others, and that wonderfully strange phrase—"it leopards the body"—served as a kind of rhythmic refrain. It is a sort of inverted cretic, by the way, to recall an old Greek meter in this new Greek narrative.

AS: I didn't know the Greek meter and am learning about it here from you. That's great.

DB: Well, I asked a classicist friend about this. That rhythm, "short long short / short long short," isn't a normative Greek meter, though just about every other triple-syllable foot is. He called it an inverted cretic, since a cretic is "long short long." Yours reverses that cadence.

AS: As a prelude to discussing the refrain, I want to say that in *Quipu* I consciously twisted nouns into verbs as part of the destabilization process. In the title poem, "Quipu," grief twists the language and turns nouns into verbs, "Loss salamanders the body, lagoons the mind." Later, there's "Did the knots of her loves jaguar in an instant?" So these unexpected twists help set up the refrain, "it leopards the body." In that section, I have white space before and after the refrain to give gravitas to it.

DB: In that phrase, what does "it" refer to? And "leopards" makes a wonderful verb—something spotted, pied, something that marks the body, or hunts it, or all of the above. How did you find that word?

AS: "It leopards the body" is used nine times in section seven. Here's the passage with the first occurrence:

> "Do-as-you're-told scum sucker, you're the reason there are
>   hydrogen bombs,"
>   yelled at the postal worker
>   behind the counter—
>
>
>   it leopards the body—

I thought the "it" might refer to the act of yelling which stains or spots the body. As each incident and refrain occurs, the "it" could refer to the preceding action, but it could also refer to a cumulative force from the world of experience. And, yes, I hoped "leopards" would mark and stain the body and make it hunted. My friend, Rikki Ducornet, once read a piece of fiction that used tiger as a verb, and I knew that someday I wanted to take another creature and turn it into a verb.

DB: The ultimate achievement of "Didyma" comes in sections nine and ten. Nine reads as a series of dependent clauses, commencing with a causal adverb "because." Section ten is, mostly, a series of independent clauses. But these sections appear on facing pages in your book, too, and this format invites us to read across the pages, across the spine, so that the clauses in nine are completed by those in ten. Thus: "Because one stirred the entrails of a goat immolated on an altar," // "nine purple irises bloom in a triangular glass vase," and so on.

That's just magnificent. The poem reads down the page, across the pages, and the effect is again to pluralize the possibilities. You make meaning out of the provisional, the accidental or random; and the coincidences of syntax and image created by the two sections becomes an additional layer of meaning.

At least that's how I read these sections. Does that comply with your sense of it all?

AS: Absolutely. The reader is indeed invited to read across the pages and connect the first phrase in section nine beginning with "because" with the first phrase in section ten, as you just did.

Yet the possibilities become even more pluralized as a reader moves through the sections. For instance, in the second set of phrases, a reader encounters "because a magpie flicks tail feathers," and then, across the page, "a pearl forms in an oyster." Can this "because" phrase actually cause the pearl to form in an oyster?

The situation becomes more complex when you look at the thirteenth phrase, "because a grain of sand lodged," and notice that it aligns with the pearl forming in an oyster. A reader is then invited to explore the relationship between causes and effects diagonally across the pages. Ultimately, because the connections don't fit in any linear way, the two sections enact a suspension of all cause and effect, or enact universal cause and effect, and a reader bathes in the totality of experience. As such, it's a fitting end to "Didyma" and to the book.

DB: All along, then, Arthur, you have been working on poetry that gives us multiple choices, layers, alternatives. Many cultures, many ways of composing, many techniques of reading, and so on.

I imagine that your twenty-two years of teaching at IAIA involved a daily juggling of multicultural things. Do you think your teaching there affected your poetry so directly?

AS: In my early years of teaching, the Institute seethed with tensions and rivalries between different Native tribes, and I found it quite a challenge.

I wasn't just juggling multicultural perspectives in class discussion. I often had to work with individual students to overcome cultural barriers and personal animosities.

At that stage, I resisted writing about my Native students, but over time, I found that my daily multicultural interactions had a growing and significant impact. In addition, I created a course, "The Poetic Image," where I showed Native students Tang dynasty Chinese poems. As I went through the poems character by character and showed students a variety of translations in English—some students then translated the poems into Native languages—it was inevitable that discussions about poetry, language, and culture sometimes clarified my own aesthetic positions and obliquely influenced my poetry.

DB: It's a very small school, as I recall, with something like two hundred and fifty students in all undergraduate degree programs. But many tribes are represented, from Inupiat in northern Alaska to Cherokee in Oklahoma. Were there common issues among the students? What kinds of special gifts—if any—did they possess as a characteristic of their backgrounds?

AS: The students often struggled with their ability to use English, but they always had a singular vitality along with a remarkable depth and diversity of lived experiences. They had a hunger and eagerness to experiment imaginatively, and those were two of their greatest strengths. In their creative writing, students were also eager to break stereotypical expectations.

DB: Do you still visit the campus?

AS: I became the first professor emeritus at the Institute in 2006, and I left with the understanding that I would keep in touch and return periodically. Each year I've returned during the fall semester to conduct a three-day residency that includes a reading, visits to poetry workshops, as well as individual conferences with creative writing majors.

DB: Are the students at IAIA inclined toward any particular kinds of poetry or particular treatments of material? More widely, what kinds of poetry do you see being written by the young these days across the country? What are their talents and what may be the challenges of the generation just emerging?

AS: The Institute students have always been willing to experiment with their writing, and their aesthetics are diverse. And that divergence, I think, is a strength in the kinds of poetry written by younger poets across the country. It's hard for me to articulate the challenges of the emerging generation—I'm confident they will do that for themselves.

DB: What are you reading these days that excites you? Are there any movements in contemporary poetry that you find notably discouraging and/or encouraging?

AS: I'm currently reading and excited by Dennis Tedlock's *Two Thousand Years of Mayan Literature* from the University of California Press. Although I'm interested in the loosely defined movement of ecopoetry, I don't want to privilege one group or movement over another. I certainly don't see myself as belonging to a movement or group, and I'd rather advocate a diversity of aesthetics. We live in a time when the complexities of our planet require a diverse array of compelling imaginative poetry. We need great poetry now more than ever before.

DB: How do you see your own poetry evolving in the near future? What are you working on, or what do you hope to work on?

AS: After completing *The Ginkgo Light* (2009), I've written a number of new poems, including the two short ones we discussed earlier in this conversation. I recently met with Susan York, a sculptor and visual artist whose work I admire, and we decided to start a collaboration. Susan's drawings appear to be minimalist—she's currently working on a series of graphite drawings where the horizon line tilts ever so slightly from drawing to drawing—but the ultimate effects are large. Back in 1989 I collaborated with Tan Dun, and we created an ensemble work that combined poetry and music, but I've never collaborated with a visual artist before.

It will be interesting to see what happens.